DATE DUE

APR 1 8 2005	
MAR 2 0 2008	
OCT 2 8 2008	
april 29, 2014	
Dec. 9, 2014	
APR 1 0 2017	
APR 2 3 2017	
DISCARD	

BRODART, CO.   Cat. No. 23-221-003

‖‖‖ ‖‖‖‖‖‖‖‖ ‖ ‖‖‖ ‖‖‖‖‖
✓ P9-EFJ-537

Are Cops Racist?

HEATHER MAC DONALD

Are Cops Racist?

CHICAGO

Ivan R. Dee

2003

Most of the contents of this book appeared originally in *City Journal*, published by The Manhattan Institute. "How the Racial Profiling Myth Helps Terrorists" is adapted from the American Enterprise Institute's December 2001 Bradley Lecture.

Library of Congress Cataloging-in-Publication Data:
  Mac Donald, Heather.
    Are cops racist? / Heather Mac Donald.
      p. cm.
    Includes index.
    ISBN 1-56663-489-X (alk. paper)
     1. Police—United States. 2. Discrimination in law enforcement—United States. 3. Racial profiling in law enforcement—United States. 4. Police-community relations—United States. 5. United States—Race relations. I. Title.

HV8141 .M23 2003
363.2'32—dc21   2002031248

Contents

Are Cops Racist?

Introduction

DEPUTY INSPECTOR James Dolan had a revolt on his hands. He nervously surveyed the angry crowd gathered at his Harlem station house, all black and Hispanic residents of the neighborhood. As precinct commander, he knew he had to say something.

"Lieutenant Quinn does live in the Bronx, you know," he tried to explain. The lieutenant himself was standing nearby, eyes downcast self-consciously.

It didn't seem to help.

And what was this all about? A protest over police brutality? Allegations of "racial profiling"?

Not quite.

John Quinn, a beloved Irish-American lieutenant, was retiring, and the people assembled at his Harlem precinct that February evening in 2001 were furious that his retirement party was being held miles away in the Bronx. "What about us?" someone shouted from the floor.

Commander Dolan finally calmed the crowd by promising a second retirement bash in Harlem. "We don't want to see you leave, Mr. Quinn," said a large, middle-aged black man wistfully. "I don't want to, either," the diminutive cop responded, in the same tone. "But time moves on."

This intensity of support for the police is common in inner-city neighborhoods across the country. But good luck finding any hint of it in the mainstream media. For the past decade the press has been on a crusade to portray cops as brutal and racist, despised by

3

the communities they are sworn to protect. That image is not just false, it is dangerous.

This book aims to tell the truth about policing—above all, about policing and race.

The last ten years should have been a time of triumph for law enforcement, not an occasion for frenzied cop-bashing. Policing got smart and produced the largest crime drop in American history: from 1991 to 1999, the nation's violent crime fell more than 25 percent. In New York City a crime-tracking process called Compstat helped drive local crime down an astounding 64 percent from 1993 to 2001. In response to the public's demand for more civil public spaces, departments started paying attention to quality-of-life offenses such as panhandling and graffiti, which also helped reduce more serious offenses.

The result was an urban renaissance nationwide. Nowhere was the link between public safety and urban vitality more dramatically evident than in New York. Gotham's police department banished fear from wide swaths of the metropolis, and the city roared back to life.

More impressive still, this conquest of crime took place as policing became more restrained and professional. Training stressed that words, not weapons, are an officer's most potent tool, and cops' use of force plummeted. Corruption, once the rule in urban departments, became the exception. Brutality was rare and highly stigmatized.

But instead of reaping accolades for their achievements, police officers found themselves under assault. For the press, so-called racial profiling became the very hallmark of policing, despite the fact that statistical evidence for such a practice is nonexistent. Aberrant tragedies, such as the 1999 shooting of Amadou Diallo by four New York City officers, became instant symbols of endemic brutality. As a cheap way to flaunt their own racial "sensitivity," politicians burdened departments with cumbersome and unneeded procedures to restrain police "bias."

For in truth the anti-police campaign was a giant exercise in denial: it was the means by which the nation's elites avoided talking about the stubborn problems of inner-city culture—above all, its greatly elevated rates of criminal behavior. If officers stop and arrest proportionately more blacks than whites, claimed the conventional dodge, it is because the cops are racist, not because blacks commit more crime. So rather than tackling the culture that produced such high rates of criminality, the nation's media and political elites campaigned to purge law enforcement of "bigotry."

Accompanying this campaign was a contemptuous dismissal of the decade's policing success. Sure, the police brought crime down, went the story, but they did so only by subjecting virtually every black citizen to incessant harassment. A young black male who hasn't been stopped and frisked without reason by overly zealous cops, claimed the anti-cop brigade, is as unlikely as a unicorn.

No part of this indictment was true. As reporters were shoving microphones in the faces of such self-anointed black spokesmen as Al Sharpton and Jesse Jackson—both guaranteed to deliver the same anti-cop message no matter the occasion—they failed to notice that law-abiding minority citizens across the country were begging for more police officers and stricter enforcement of the laws.

Go to any inner-city police-community meeting and the first thing you will hear is, "Why aren't you arresting the drug dealers on the corners?"—not "Why are you abusing us?" The *New York Times* has sent scores of reporters out to cover police-community relations, but they never seem to find people like the Reverend Terry Lee, a young Jamaican preacher in Brooklyn. The police do "great work," he told me emphatically. "They allow our senior citizens to walk to the market; they patrol when we are sleeping; they're on our block watching for us." Lee speaks for the silent majority of inner-city residents who see the police as their guardians and have only contempt for anti-cop agitators.

The press and liberal activists ignore such opinions, just as they ignore the views of black officers who debunk the "racial profiling" charge. My purpose in the following pages is to expose the prevailing account of policing as myth, by reporting directly from inner-city neighborhoods, by asking police officers how they actually do their jobs—something almost no reporter or so-called rights advocate has ever bothered to do—and by exposing the cop-bashers' flagrant misuse of statistics. The anti-cop crusade dominates national discussion at such flash-point moments as the 1999 Amadou Diallo protests or the 2001 Cincinnati riots. By reconstructing these episodes, I hope to show how the race industry and the opinion elites routinely impose cookie-cutter stories of racist policing on far more complicated realities.

Before the 1990s the racial rap against cops was that they ignored crime in black neighborhoods. Thankfully such neglect is a thing of the past. But the irony of contemporary policing is that cops today face the reverse dilemma: if they respond to inner-city residents' heartfelt call for protection, they may well leave themselves open to charges of racism. The mandates that have metastasized across the country, requiring police departments to record the race of every person they stop, search, or arrest, raise a presumption of bias against individual officers—or entire departments—if their stop-and-arrest data do not exactly mirror the racial composition of the local population. Like the entire anti-profiling crusade, such a conclusion rests on a breathtaking ignorance of policing strategies—including, among other relevant factors, the many behavioral cues that actually lead an officer to stop someone. Yet these mandates are convincing many officers that fighting crime aggressively is not worth risking a career-destroying bias charge.

The most immediate casualties will be in the inner city, but the damage from anti-cop activism may not remain so localized. Local police are our first line of defense against terrorism; they, not federal agents, are most likely to encounter the terrorists already among us. If officers fear that aggressively tracking down terrorist leads or acting on reasonable suspicion will bring on charges of discrimination, our entire society is in danger.

Is policing perfect? Is every cop a gentleman? Of course not. But rogue officers by no means represent the profession as a whole. Unless the country pulls back—and fast—from its scapegoating of the police, it will soon find the public safety gains of the last decade melting away.

Despite this concern, this is ultimately an optimistic book. The most striking thing about hearing black and white officers describe their work is how alike they sound. I found over and over again an indistinguishable commitment to the rule of law and a belief in color-blind justice, not the deep perceptual divide that race hustlers and academic charlatans claim is the American reality. Long before September 11 restored some moral clarity to our national discourse, police officers saw the world in terms of good and evil, not skin color. They still do. "People in prison are not black or white—they're criminals," a black police chief told me. The people in crime-riddled communities from Harlem to Oakland know this too.

The Myth of Racial Profiling

THE ANTI–"RACIAL PROFILING" JUGGERNAUT must be stopped before it obliterates the crime-fighting gains of the last decade, especially in inner cities. The anti-profiling crusade thrives on an ignorance of policing and a willful blindness to the demographics of crime. Yet politicians are swarming on board. President George W. Bush has joined the rush, declaring portentously: "Racial profiling is wrong, and we will end it in America."

Too bad no one asked President Bush, "What exactly do you mean by 'racial profiling,' and what evidence do you have that it exists?" For the anti-profiling crusaders have created a headlong movement without defining their central term and without providing a shred of credible evidence that "racial profiling" is a widespread police practice.

The ultimate question in the profiling controversy is whether the disproportionate involvement of blacks and Hispanics with law enforcement reflects police racism or the consequences of disproportionate minority crime. Anti-profiling activists hope to make police racism an all but irrebuttable presumption whenever enforcement statistics show high rates of minority stops and arrests. But not so fast.

Two meanings of "racial profiling" intermingle in the activists'

9

rhetoric. What we may call "hard" profiling uses race as the only factor in assessing criminal suspiciousness: an officer sees a black person and, without more to go on, pulls him over for a pat-down on the chance that he may be carrying drugs or weapons. "Soft" racial profiling uses race as one factor among others in gauging criminal suspiciousness: the highway police, for example, have intelligence that Jamaican drug posses with a fondness for Nissan Pathfinders are transporting marijuana along the northeast corridor. A New Jersey trooper sees a black motorist speeding in a Pathfinder and pulls him over in the hope of finding drugs.

The racial profiling debate focuses primarily on highway stops. The police are pulling over a disproportionate number of minority drivers for traffic offenses, goes the argument, in order to look for drugs. Sure, the driver committed an infraction, but the reason the trooper chose to stop him, rather than the speeder next to him, was his race.

But the profiling critics also fault both the searches that sometimes follow a highway stop and the tactics of urban policing. Any evaluation of the evidence for, and the appropriateness of, the use of race in policing must keep these contexts distinct. Highway *stops* should almost always be color-blind, I'll argue, but in other policing environments (including highway *searches*), where an officer has many clues to go on, race may be among them. Ironically, effective urban policing shows that the more additional factors an officer has access to in his criminal profile, the more valid race becomes—and the less significant, almost to the point of irrelevance.

Before reviewing the evidence that profiling critics offer, recall the demands that the police face every day, far from anti-police agitators and their journalist acolytes.

February 22, 2001, a town-hall meeting at P.S. 153 in Harlem between New York mayor Rudolph Giuliani and Harlem residents: A woman sarcastically asks Giuliani if police officers downtown are paid more than uptown officers, "because we don't have any quality of life in Harlem, none whatsoever. Drug dealers are allowed to stand out in front of our houses every day, to practically invade us, and nothing's done about it." Another woman complains that dealers are back on the street the day after being arrested, and notes that "addicts are so bold that we have to get off the sidewalk and go around them!" She calls for the declaration of a state of emergency. A man wonders if cop-basher congressman Charles Rangel, present at the meeting, could "endow the police with more power," and suggests that the NYPD coordinate with the federal Drug Enforcement Administration, the INS, and the IRS to bring order to the streets.

The audience meets Giuliani's assertions that the police have brought crime down sharply in Harlem with hoots of derision. No one mentions "police brutality."

Valentine's Day, 2001, a police-community meeting at Harlem's 28th Precinct: An elegant man in an angora turtleneck, tiny blue glasses, and a shadow of a goatee breaks a local taboo by asking what the precinct is doing "to address dealing on the corners." Most residents shrink from mentioning the problem at precinct meetings for fear of retaliation from dealers. A tense silence falls. The man, a restaurant investor, tells me, "If this was 59th and Park, the police wouldn't allow these individuals to hang out on the corner." He can't understand why there's no "immediate result" if the police have in fact been cracking down on drug-dealing. "I don't think it should be so hard to dismantle," he says impatiently.

February 12, 2001, the fifth floor of a hulking yellow apartment building on Lenox Road in Flatbush, Brooklyn: Two officers from the 67th Precinct investigate an anonymous call reporting a group of youths smoking marijuana in the hallway. The boys have disappeared. As officers check the stairwell, a gaunt middle-aged man sporting a wildly patterned black-and-white tie courteously introduces himself as Mr. Johnson, the building superintendent. After slowly bending down to pick up a discarded cigarette butt, he asks politely if anything more can be done about the kids who come from the next building to smoke pot in his hallway.

This is the demand—often angry, sometimes wistful—that urban police forces constantly hear: get rid of the drugs! These recent appeals come after the most successful war on crime that New York City has ever conducted. A decade and a half ago, when drug-related drive-by shootings became epidemic, inner-city residents nationwide were calling even more frantically for protection from drug violence. When New Jersey, a key state on the drug corridor from Central America to New England, sent its state highway troopers to do foot patrols in Camden and Trenton, residents met them with cheers.

In New York the mayhem eventually led to the development of the Giuliani administration's assertive policing that strives, quite successfully, to prevent crime from happening. Outside of New York the widespread pleas to stop drug violence led the Drug Enforcement Administration to enlist state highway police in their anti-drug efforts. The DEA and the Customs Service had been using intelligence about drug routes and the typical itineraries of couriers to interdict drugs at airports; now the interdiction war would expand to the nation's highways, the major artery of the cocaine trade.

The DEA taught state troopers some common identifying signs of drug couriers: nervousness; conflicting information about origin and destination cities among vehicle occupants; no luggage for a long trip; lots of cash; lack of a driver's license or insurance; the spare tire in the backseat; rental license plates or plates from key source states like Arizona and New Mexico; loose screws or scratches near a vehicle's hollow spaces, which can be converted to hiding places for drugs and guns. The agency also shared intelligence about the types of cars that couriers favored on certain routes, as well as about the ethnic makeup of drug-trafficking organizations. A typical DEA report from the early 1990s noted that "large-scale interstate trafficking networks controlled by

Jamaicans, Haitians, and black street gangs dominate the manufacture and distribution of crack." The 1999 "Heroin Trends" report out of Newark declared that "predominant wholesale traffickers are Colombian, followed by Dominicans, Chinese, West African/ Nigerian, Pakistani, Hispanic and Indian. Mid-levels are dominated by Dominicans, Colombians, Puerto Ricans, African-Americans and Nigerians."

According to the racial profiling crowd, the war on drugs immediately became a war on minorities, on the highways and off. Their alleged evidence for racial profiling comes in two varieties: anecdotal, which is of limited value; and statistical, which on examination proves entirely worthless.

Black motorists today almost routinely claim that the only reason they are pulled over for highway stops is their race. Once they are pulled over, they say, they are subject to harassment, including traumatic searches. Some of these tales are undoubtedly true. Without question there are obnoxious officers out there, and some officers may ignore their training and target minorities. But since the advent of video cameras in patrol cars, installed in the wake of the racial profiling controversy, most charges of police racism, testified to under oath, have been disproved as lies.

The allegation that police systematically single out minorities for unjustified law enforcement ultimately stands or falls on numbers. In suits against police departments across the country, the ACLU and the Justice Department have waved studies aplenty allegedly demonstrating selective enforcement. None of them holds up to scrutiny.

The typical study purports to show that minority motorists are subject to disproportionate traffic stops. Trouble is, no one yet has devised an adequate benchmark against which to measure if police are pulling over, searching, or arresting "too many" blacks and Hispanics. The question must always be: too many compared with what? Even anti-profiling activists generally concede that police pull drivers over for an actual traffic violation, not for no reason whatsoever, so a valid benchmark for stops would be the number of serious traffic violators, not just drivers. If it turns out that minorities tend to drive more recklessly, say, or have more equipment violations, you'd expect them to be subject to more stops. But to benchmark accurately, you'd also need to know the number of miles driven by different racial groups, so that you'd compare stops per man-mile, not just per person. Throw in age demographics as well: if a minority group has more young people—read: immature drivers—than whites do, expect more traffic stops of that group. The final analysis must then compare police deployment patterns with racial driving patterns: if more police are on the road when a higher proportion of blacks are driving—on weekend nights, say—stops of blacks will rise.

No traffic-stop study to date comes near the requisite sophistication. Most simply compare the number of minority stops with some crude population measure, and all contain huge and fatal data gaps. An ACLU analysis of Philadelphia traffic stops, for example, merely used the percentage of blacks in the 1990 census as a benchmark for stops made seven years later. In about half the stops the ACLU studied, the officer did not record the race of the motorist. The study ignored the rate of traffic violations by race, so its grand conclusion of selective enforcement is meaningless.

Only two studies, both by Temple University social psychologist John Lamberth, have attempted to create a violator benchmark. The ACLU used one to sue, successfully, the Maryland state police; a criminal defense attorney in New Jersey used the other to free seventeen accused black drug traffickers. Lamberth alleged that blacks in Maryland and southern New Jersey were stopped at higher rates than their representation in the violator population would seemingly warrant. But he defined violator so broadly—in Maryland, traveling at least one mile, and in New Jersey, traveling at least six miles, over the speed limit—that he included virtually the entire driving population. Lamberth must not have spent much time talking to real cops, for his definition of violator ignores how police actually decide whom to stop. Someone gliding sedately at fifty-six miles an hour in a fifty-five-mile-an-hour zone has a radically different chance of being pulled over than someone barreling along at eighty. An adequate benchmark must capture the kind of driving likely to draw police attention. Despite his severely flawed methodology, Lamberth is in great demand as a racial profiling guru.

Do minorities commit more of the kinds of traffic violations that police target? This is a taboo question among the racial profiling crowd; to ask it is to reveal one's racism. No one has studied it. But some evidence suggests that it may be the case. The National Highway Traffic Safety Administration found that blacks were 10 percent of drivers nationally, 13 percent of drivers in fatal accidents, and 16 percent of drivers in injury accidents. (Lower rates of seat-belt use may contribute to these numbers.) Random national surveys of drivers on weekend nights in 1973, 1986, and 1996 found that blacks were more likely to fail Breathalyzer tests than whites. In Illinois, blacks have a higher motorist fatality rate than whites. Blacks in one New Jersey study were 23 percent of all drivers arrested at the scene of an accident for driving drunk, though only 13.5 percent of highway users. In San Diego, blacks have more accidents than their population figures would predict. Hispanics get in a disproportionate number of accidents nationally.

But though the numbers to date are incapable of telling us anything about racial profiling, that does not mean that it was not going on in some locations, at some times. Hard racial profiling in car stops—pulling over one speeder among many just because he happens to be black or Hispanic—has surely been rare. But conversations with officers in strong interdiction states such as New Jersey suggest that some troopers probably did practice soft racial profiling—pulling someone over because driver and car and direction and number and type of occupants fit the components of a drug courier profile.

Over time, officers' experience had corroborated the DEA intelligence reports: minorities were carrying most of the drugs. An example of the patterns they noticed: a group of young blacks with North Carolina plates traveling south out of Manhattan's Lincoln Tunnel into New Jersey? Good chance they're carrying weapons and drugs, having just made a big buy in the city. Catch them northbound? Good chance they're carrying big money and guns. Some officers inevitably started playing the odds—how many, the numbers cannot yet tell us.

Despite the hue and cry, there is nothing illegal about using race as one factor among others in assessing criminal suspiciousness. Nevertheless the initial decision to pull a car over should be based almost always on seriousness of traffic violation alone—unless, of course, evidence of other lawbreaking, such as drug use, is visible. If the result is that drug couriers assiduously observe the speed limit, fine. But compared with most other policing environments, highways are relatively cueless places. In assessing the potential criminality of a driver speeding along with the pack on an eight-lane highway, an officer normally has much less to work with than on a city street or sidewalk. His locational cues—traveling on an interstate pointed toward a drug market, say—are crude compared with those in a city, where an officer can ask if this particular block is a drug bazaar. His ability to observe the behavior of a suspect over time is limited by the speed of travel. In such an environment, blacks traveling seventy-eight miles an hour should not face a greater chance of getting pulled over than white speeders just because they are black and happen to be driving a car said to be favored by drug mules.

Soft racial profiling was probably not widespread enough to have influenced traffic-stop rates significantly. Nor will eliminating it quickly change the belief among many blacks that any time they get stopped for a traffic violation, it is because of their race. Nevertheless state police commanders should eliminate any contribution that soft profiling may make to that perception, unless strong evidence emerges (as it has not so far) that soft profiling has had an extremely high success rate in drug interdiction. Far more is at stake here than the use of race in traffic stops. Specious anti–racial profiling analysis threatens to emasculate policing in areas where drug enforcement is on a far stronger basis.

The most important victory of the anti–racial profiling agitators occurred not on the traffic-stop battlefield but on the very different terrain of the searches that sometimes follow a stop. And here is where people who care about law enforcement should really start to worry. On April 20, 1999, New Jersey's then–attorney general Peter Verniero issued his "Interim Report of the State Police Review Team Regarding Allegations of Racial Profiling." It was a bombshell, whose repercussions haven't stopped yet.

"The problem of disparate treatment [of blacks] is real, not imagined," the report famously declared. Governor Christine Todd Whitman chimed in: "There is no question that racial profiling exists at some level." The media triumphantly broadcast the findings as conclusive proof of racial profiling not just in the Garden State but nationally. The *New York Times* started regularly referring to New Jersey's "racial bias" on the highways as incontrovertible fact. Defense attorneys and their clients celebrated as well. "Whenever I have a state police case, I file a suppression motion . . . alleging that the stop was based on color of skin and therefore illegal," a Trenton criminal defense attorney told the *New York Times*. "And now guess what? The state agrees with me!"

Yet the report's influential analysis is shoddy beyond belief. Contrary to popular perception, Verniero did not reach any conclusions about racial profiling in stops. His finding of "disparate treatment" is based on the percentage of "consent searches" performed on minorities after a stop has occurred. (In a consent search, the motorist agrees to allow the trooper to search his car and person without a warrant or probable cause.) Between 1994 and 1998, claims the report, 53 percent of consent searches on the southern end of the New Jersey Turnpike involved a black person, 21 percent involved whites, and overall 77 percent involved minorities. But these figures are meaningless, because Verniero does not include racial information about search requests that were denied, and his report mixes stops, searches, and arrests from different time periods.

But most important: Verniero finds culpable racial imbalance in the search figures without suggesting a proper benchmark. He simply assumes that 53 percent black consent searches is too high. Compared with what? If blacks in fact carry drugs at a higher rate than do whites, then this search rate merely reflects good law enforcement. If the police are now to be accused of racism every time they go where the crime is, that's the end of public safety.

The hue and cry over the alleged New Jersey search rate makes sense only if we assume that drug trafficking is spread evenly across the entire population and that officers are unable to detect the signs of a courier once they have pulled over a car. There are powerful reasons to reject both these assumptions.

Judging by arrest rates, minorities are vastly overrepresented among drug traffickers. Blacks make up more than 60 percent of arrests in New Jersey for drugs and weapons, though they are 13.5 percent of the population. Against such a benchmark, the state police search rates look proportionate.

The attorney general's report dismissed this comparison with an argument that has become de rigueur among the anti–racial profiling crowd, even in Congress: the "circularity" argument. Arrest and conviction data for drugs and weapons are virtually meaningless, said Verniero. They tell you nothing about the world and everything about the false stereotypes that guide the police. If the police find more contraband on blacks and Hispanics, that is merely because they are looking harder for it, driven by prejudiced assumptions. If the police were to target whites with as much enforcement zeal, goes this reasoning, they would find comparable levels of criminality. David Harris, a University of Toledo law school professor and the leading expert for the anti-profiling forces, makes this preposterous argument. An enforcement effort directed at forty-year-old white law professors, he assures a Senate subcommittee, would yield noticeable busts. The disproportionate minority arrests then reinforce the initial, racist stereotypes, and the vicious cycle begins all over again—too many minorities arrested, too many whites going free.

The circularity argument is an insult to law enforcement and a prime example of the anti-police advocates' willingness to rewrite reality. Though it is hard to prove a negative—in this case, that there is not a large cadre of white drug lords operating in the inner cities—circumstantial evidence rebuts the activists' insinuation. Between 1976 and 1994, 64 percent of the homicide victims in drug turf wars were black, according to a Heritage Foundation analysis of FBI data. Sixty-seven percent of known perpetrators were also black. Likewise, some 60 percent of victims and perpetrators in drug-induced fatal brawls are black. These figures match the roughly 60 percent of drug offenders in state prison who are black. Unless you believe that white traffickers are less violent than black traffickers, the arrest, conviction, and imprisonment rate for blacks on drug charges appears consistent with the level of drug activity in the black population. (And were it true that white dealers are less violent, wouldn't we expect police to concentrate their enforcement efforts on the most dangerous parts of the drug trade?)

The notion that there are lots of heavy-duty white dealers sneaking by undetected contradicts the street experience of just about every narcotics cop you will ever talk to—though such anecdotal evidence, of course, would fail to convince the ACLU, convinced as it is of the blinding racism that afflicts most officers. "The hard-core sellers are where the hard-core users are—places like 129th Street in Harlem," observes Patrick Harnett, retired chief of the narcotics division for the NYPD. "It's not white kids from Rockland County who are keeping black sellers in business."

The cops go where the deals are. When white club owners, along with Israelis and Russians, still dominated the Ecstasy trade, that's whom the cops were arresting. Recently, however, big shipments have been going to minority neighborhoods; subsequent arrests will reflect crime intelligence, not racism.

There's not a single narcotics officer who won't freely admit that there are cocaine buys going down in the men's bathrooms of Wall Street investment firms—though at a small fraction of the amount found on 129th Street. But that is not where community outrage, such as that Mayor Giuliani heard in Harlem, is directing the police, because they don't produce violence and street intimidation.

Ultimately the circularity argument rests on a massive denial of reality, one that is remarkably vigorous and widespread. In March 2000, for example, New Jersey senator Robert Torricelli asserted before then-Senator John Ashcroft's Judiciary Subcommittee: "Statistically it cannot bear evidence [sic] to those who suggest, as our former superintendent of the state police suggested, that certain ethnic or racial groups disproportionately commit crimes. They do not." Needless to say, Torricelli provided no statistics.

The second condition necessary to explain the higher minority search rates on the highway is patrol officers' ability to detect drug trafficking. Unlike the initial decision to pull over a car, the decision to request permission to search rests on a wealth of cues. One of the most frequent is conflicting narratives among passengers and driver. "If a group in a car is carrying drugs, there will always be inconsistencies in their stories," reports Ed Lennon, head of the New Jersey Troopers Union. "It's unbelievable. A lot of times the driver won't know the passengers' first or last names—'I only know him as Bill'—or they'll get the names completely wrong. Sometimes they'll have a preplanned answer regarding their destination, but their purpose in being on the road will vary."

A driver's demeanor may also be a tip-off. "I've stopped white guys in pickup trucks with a camper compartment on top," recalls Lennon. "Their chest is pounding; they're sweating, though it's the dead of winter. They won't look at you." And they're also hiding drugs.

Once a trooper stops a car, he can see the amount of luggage and its fit with the alleged itinerary, the accumulation of trash that suggests long stretches without stopping, the signs of drug use, the lack of a license and registration, the single key in the ignition and no trunk key, or the signs that the vehicle may have been fitted out with drug and weapon compartments. Some New York narcotics officers recently pulled over an Azusa SUV and noticed welding marks along the rain gutter on top. The occupants had raised the entire roof four inches to create a drug vault. If a car's windows don't roll all the way down, drugs may be concealed in the doors.

The fact that hit rates for contraband tend to be equal across racial groups, even though blacks and Hispanics are searched at higher rates, suggests that the police are successfully targeting dealers, not minorities. Race may play a role in that targeting, or it may not. Most cues of trafficking are race-neutral; it may be that race often correlates with the decision to search rather than causing it. But if race does play a role in the request to search, it is a much diminished one compared with a car stop based on a courier profile. When an officer has many independent indices of suspicion, adding his knowledge of the race of major trafficking groups to the mix is both legitimate and not overly burdensome on law-abiding minorities.

Amazingly, Attorney General Verniero acknowledges that the police merely try to maximize their hit rates in deciding whom to search, but he blames them for doing so. "The state police reward system gave practical impetus to the use of these inappropriate stereotypes about drug dealers" by rewarding big busts, he frets. But if the police were seeking to maximize their contraband yields, and the alleged "inappropriate stereotypes" were not helping them do so, presumably they would abandon those "stereotypes" and find some other set of cues—unless, of course, they were merely out to harass minorities for the thrill of it. But in that case their hit rates would be lower for minorities than for whites, which they were not.

The bottom line is this: the New Jersey attorney general has branded the state police as racist without a scintilla of analysis for his finding. Yet New Jersey is the wave of the future, for racial profiling data-collection initiatives are sweeping the country. At least thirty states could soon require their state police to collect racial data on all traffic stops and searches, with the stated end of eliminating "racial profiling." Urban forces are under identical pressure. Virtually every major law-enforcement organization opposes these bills, because of their failure to deal with the benchmarking problem. Until someone devises an adequately sophisticated benchmark that takes into account population patterns on the roads, degrees of lawbreaking, police deployment patterns, and the nuances of police decision making, stop data are as meaningless as they are politically explosive. Attorney General John Ashcroft has encouraged these data-gathering initiatives; he should instead withhold his support unless local proponents can prove that they will capture the complex realities of law enforcement.

Unfortunately the flurry of racial profiling analysis is not confined to the highways. It will wreak the most havoc on urban policing. Despite the racket by protesters, it is in city policing that race probably plays its least significant role, because officers have so many other cues from the environment. In assessing whether a pedestrian is behaving suspiciously, for example, they might already know that he is at a drug corner, about which they have received numerous complaints. They know if there has been a string of burglaries in the neighborhood. As they observe him, they can assess with whom he is interacting, and how.

A New York Street Crime Unit sergeant in Queens describes having stopped white pedestrians who had immediately changed directions as soon as they saw his unmarked car or ducked into an alley or a store for eight seconds and then looked for him once they came out. The night I spoke to him he was patrolling the 102nd Precinct in Woodhaven, a largely white and Hispanic neighborhood. He had earlier questioned a white kid hanging out in front of a factory. "He was breaking his neck looking back at us; we thought he was a burglar." It turns out he was waiting for a friend. Another night in another precinct, the sergeant saw two black kids on bikes. "One guy's arm was hanging straight down, like he was carrying a gun. When they saw us, the other guy took off on his bike and threw a bag away. It was felony-weight drugs." Are you ignoring whites with guns? I asked him. "Of course not; I could see the same thing tonight," he said impatiently. "I don't use race at all. The only question is: are you raising my level of suspicion? Fifteen minutes after a stop, I may not even be able to tell you the color of the guy."

Even car stops on city streets usually have more context than on a highway. "If we pass four or five guys in a car going the opposite direction," explains the Queens sergeant, "and they're all craning their necks to see if we notice them, we may reverse and follow them for a while. We won't pull them over, but our suspicion is up. We'll run their plates. If the plates don't check out, they're done. If they commit a traffic violation, we won't pull everyone out of the car yet; we'll just interview the driver. If he doesn't have paperwork, it may be a stolen car. Now everyone's coming out to be frisked."

Hard as it is to believe, criminals actually do keep turning around to look at officers, though it would seem an obvious giveaway. "Thank God they're stupid, or we'd be out of a job," the sergeant laughs.

But urban policing depends on another race-neutral strength: it is data-driven. The greatest recent innovation in policing was New York's Compstat, the computer-generated crime analysis that allows police commanders to pinpoint their enforcement efforts, then allows top brass to hold them accountable for results. If robberies are up in Bushwick, Brooklyn, the precinct commander will strategically deploy his officers to find the perpetrators. Will all the suspects be black? Quite likely, for so is the neighborhood. Does that mean that the officers are racist? Hardly; they are simply going where the crime is. In most high-crime neighborhoods, race is wholly irrelevant to policing, because nearly all the residents are minorities.

Urban police chiefs worry about the data-collection mania as much as highway patrol commanders do. Ed Flynn, chief of police for Virginia's Arlington County, explains why. Last year the black community in his jurisdiction was demanding heavier drug enforcement. "We had a series of community meetings. The residents said to us: 'Years ago, you had control over the problem. Now the kids are starting to act out again.' They even asked us: 'Where are your jump-out squads [who observe drug deals from their cars, then jump out and nab the participants]?'" So Flynn and his local commander put together an energetic strategy to break up the drug trade. They instituted aggressive motor-vehicle checks throughout the problem neighborhood. Cracked windshield, too-dark windows, expired tags, driving too fast? You're getting stopped and questioned. "We wanted to increase our presence in the area and make it quite unpleasant for the dealers to operate," Flynn says. The Arlington officers also cracked down on quality-of-life offenses like public urination, and used undercover surveillance to take out the dealers.

By the end of the summer the department had cleaned up the crime hot spots. Community newsletters thanked the cops for breaking up the dealing. But guess what? Says Flynn: "We had also just generated a lot of data showing 'disproportionate' minority arrests." The irony, in Flynn's view, is acute. "We are responding to heartfelt demands for increased police presence," he says. "But this places police departments in the position of producing data at the community's behest that can be used against them."

The racial profiling analysis profoundly confuses cause and effect. "Police develop tactics in response to the disproportionate victimization of minorities by minorities, and you are calling the tactics the problem?" Flynn marvels.

However much the racial profilers try to divert attention away from the facts of crime, those facts remain obdurate. Arlington has a 10 percent black population, but robbery victims identify nearly 70 percent of their assailants as black. In 1998 blacks in New York City were thirteen times more likely than whites to commit a violent assault, according to victim reports. As long as those numbers remain unchanged, police statistics will also look disproportionate. This is the crime problem that black leaders should be shouting about.

But the politics of racial profiling has taken over everything else. Here again New Jersey is a model of profiling pandering, and it foreshadows the irrationality that will beset the rest of the country. In February 1999 New Jersey governor Christine Todd Whitman peremptorily fired the head of the state police, Colonel Carl Williams, whose reputation for honesty had earned him the nickname "The Truth." It was the truth that got him fired. The day before his dismissal, Williams had had the temerity to tell a newspaper reporter that minority groups dominate the cocaine and marijuana trade.

Of course, this information had constituted the heart of DEA reports for years. No matter. Stating it publicly violated some collective fairy tale that all groups commit drug crimes at equal rates. Whitman's future political career depended on getting Williams's head, and she got it.

One way to make sure that nasty confrontations with the facts about crime don't happen again is to stop publishing those facts. And so the New Jersey state police no longer distribute a typical felony-offender profile to their officers, because such profiles may contribute, in the attorney general's words, to "inappropriate stereotypes" about criminals. Never mind that in law enforcement, with its deadly risk, more information is always better than less. Expect calls for the barring of racial information from crime analysis to spread nationally.

The New Jersey attorney general's office has also dropped its appeal of a devastating 1996 trial court decision that had declared the state police guilty of "institutional racism." Using Lamberth's

New Jersey traffic study as proof of racial profiling, the court dismissed drug indictments against seventeen blacks without so much as glancing at the facts of their cases. The court was wrong on the evidence and wrong on the law, but the case now stands permanently on the books as the most important judicial decision to date on racial profiling.

Next the New Jersey attorney general himself dismissed en masse drug and weapons charges against 128 defendants. The defendants all alleged that state troopers had pulled them over merely because of race. The attorney general was not willing to defend the state's officers and so let the defendants go free. In one case, the defendants' car allegedly passed a marked cruiser at seventy-five miles an hour; the occupants were openly smoking pot and drinking; the trooper found cocaine—hardly a case of racial profiling, hard or soft. Numerous requests to the attorney general's office for comment on the case have gone unanswered.

New Jersey will soon monitor the length of traffic stops that individual officers make and correlate it to the race of the motorist. It will also monitor by race the computer checks that individual officers run on license plates, on the theory that racist officers will spend more time bothering innocent black motorists and will improperly target them for background checks. Of course an officer's stop and arrest data will be closely scrutinized for racial patterns as well. And if in fact such investigatory techniques correlate with race because more minorities are breaking the law? Too bad for the cop. He will be red-flagged as a potential racist.

These programs monitoring individual officers are present in all jurisdictions that, like New Jersey, operate under a federal monitor. Along with the new state requirements for racial data collection on a department-wide basis, they will destroy assertive policing, for they penalize investigatory work. The political classes are telling police officers that if they have "too many" enforcement interactions with minorities, it is because they are racists. Officers are responding by cutting back enforcement. Drug arrests dropped 55 percent on the Garden State Parkway in New Jersey in 2000, and 25 percent on the turnpike and parkway combined. When the mayor and the police chief of Minneapolis accused Minneapolis officers of racial profiling, traffic stops dropped 63 percent. Pittsburgh officers, under a federal consent decree monitoring their individual enforcement actions, now report they are arresting by racial quota. Arrests in Los Angeles, whose police department has been under fire from the Justice Department, dropped 25 percent in the first nine months of 2000, while homicides jumped 25 percent.

The Harlem residents who so angrily demanded more drug busts from Mayor Giuliani last February didn't care about the race of the criminals who were destroying their neighborhood. They didn't see "black" or "white." They only saw dealers—and they wanted them out. That is precisely the perspective of most police officers as well; their world is divided into "good people" and "bad people," not into this race or that.

If the racial profiling crusade shatters this commonality between law-abiding inner-city residents and the police, it will be just those law-abiding minorities who will pay the heaviest price.

2001

Sorry, No Debunking of Racial Profiling Allowed

THE ANTI—RACIAL PROFILING JUGGERNAUT has finally met its nemesis: the truth. According to a new study, black drivers on the New Jersey Turnpike are twice as likely to speed as white drivers, and are even more dominant among drivers breaking ninety miles an hour. This finding demolishes the myth of racial profiling. Precisely for that reason, the Bush Justice Department tried to bury the report so the profiling juggernaut could continue its destructive campaign against law enforcement. What happens next will show whether the politics of racial victimization now trump all other national concerns.

Until now the anti-police crusade that travels under the banner of "ending racial profiling" has traded on ignorance. Its spokesmen went around the country charging that the police were stopping "too many" minorities for traffic infractions or more serious violations. The reason, explained the anti-cop crowd, was that the police were racist.

They can argue that no more. The new turnpike study, commissioned by the New Jersey attorney general, solves one of the most vexing problems in racial profiling analysis: establishing a violator benchmark. To show that the police are stopping "too many" members of a group, you need to know, at a minimum, the rate of lawbreaking among that group—the so-called violator benchmark. Only if the rate of stops or arrests greatly exceeds the rate of criminal behavior should our suspicions be raised. But most of the studies that the ACLU and defense attorneys have proffered to show biased behavior by the police have used only crude population measures as the benchmark for comparing police activity—arguing, say, that if 24 percent of speeding stops on a particular stretch of highway were of black drivers, in a city or state where blacks make up 19 percent of the population, the police are overstopping blacks.

Such an analysis is clearly specious, since it fails to say what percentage of speeders are black, but the data required to rebut it were not available. Matthew Zingraff, a criminologist at North Carolina State University, explains why: "Everybody was terrified. Good statisticians were throwing up their hands and saying, 'This is one battle you'll never win. I don't want to be called a racist.'" Even to suggest studying the driving behavior of different racial groups was to demonstrate one's bigotry, as Zingraff himself discovered when he proposed such research in North Carolina and promptly came under attack. Such investigations violate the reigning fiction in anti–racial profiling rhetoric: that all groups commit crime and other infractions at equal rates. It follows from this central fiction that any differences in the rate at which the police interact with certain citizens result only from police bias, not from differences in citizen behavior.

Despite the glaring flaws in every racial profiling study heretofore available, the press and the politicians jumped on the anti-profiling bandwagon. How could they lose? They showed their racial sensitivity, and as for defaming the police without evidence, well, you don't have to worry that the *New York Times* will be on your case if you do.

No institution made more destructive use of racial profiling junk science than the Clinton Justice Department. Armed with the shoddy studies, it slapped costly consent decrees on police departments across the country, requiring them to monitor their officers' every interaction with minorities, among other managerial intrusions.

No consent decree was more precious to the anti-police agenda than the one slapped on New Jersey. In 1999 then-Governor Christine Todd Whitman had declared her state's highway troopers guilty of racial profiling, based on a study of consent searches that would earn an F in a freshman statistics class. (In a highway consent search, an officer asks a driver for permission to search his car, usually for drugs or weapons.) The study, executed by the New Jersey attorney general, lacked crucial swaths of data on stops, searches, and arrests, and compensated for the lack by mixing data from wildly different time periods. Most fatally, the attorney general's study lacked any benchmark of the rate at which different racial groups transport illegal drugs on the turnpike. Its conclusion that the New Jersey state troopers were searching "too many" blacks for drugs was therefore meaningless.

Hey, no problem! exclaimed the Clinton Justice Department. Here's your consent decree and high-priced federal monitor; we'll expect a lengthy report every three months on your progress in combating your officers' bigotry.

Universally decried as racists, New Jersey's troopers started shunning discretionary law-enforcement activity. Consent searches on the turnpike, which totaled 440 in 1999, the year the anti–racial profiling campaign got in full swing, dropped to an astoundingly low 11 in the six months that ended October 31, 2001. At the height of the drug war in 1988, the troopers filed 7,400 drug charges from the turnpike, most of those from consent searches; in 2000 they filed 370 drug charges, a number that doubtless has been steadily dropping since then. It is unlikely that drug trafficking has dropped on New Jersey's main highway by anything like these percentages.

"There's a tremendous demoralizing effect of being guilty until proven innocent," explains trooper union vice president Dave Jones. "Anyone you interact with can claim you've made a race-based stop, and you spend years defending yourself." Arrests by state troopers have also been plummeting since the Whitman–Justice Department racial profiling declaration. Not surprisingly, murder jumped 65 percent in Newark, a major destination of drug traffickers, between 2000 and 2001. In an eerie replay of the eighties' drug battles, Camden is considering inviting the state police back to fight its homicidal drug gangs.

But one thing did not change after the much-publicized consent decree: the proportion of blacks stopped on the turnpike for speeding continued to exceed their proportion in the driving population. Man, those troopers must be either really dumb or really racist! thought most observers, including the New Jersey attorney general, who accused the troopers of persistent profiling.

Faced with constant calumny for their stop rates, the New Jersey troopers asked the attorney general to do the unthinkable: study speeding behavior on the turnpike. If it turned out that all groups drive the same, as the reigning racial profiling myths hold, then the troopers would accept the consequences.

Well, we now know that the troopers were neither dumb nor racist; they were merely doing their jobs. According to the study commissioned by the New Jersey attorney general and leaked first to the *New York Times* and then to the Internet, blacks make up 16 percent of the drivers on the turnpike and 25 percent of the speeders in the sixty-five-mile-an-hour zones, where profiling complaints are most common. (The study counted only those going more than fifteen miles an hour over the speed limit as speeders.) Black drivers speed twice as much as white drivers, and speed at reckless levels even more. Blacks are actually stopped less than their speeding behavior would predict—they are 23 percent of those stopped.

The devastation wrought by this study to the anti-police agenda is catastrophic. The medieval Vatican could not have been more threatened had Galileo offered photographic proof of the solar system. It turns out that the police stop blacks more for speeding because they speed more. Race has nothing to do with it.

This is not a politically acceptable result. And the researchers who conducted the study knew it. Anticipating a huge backlash should they go public with their findings, they checked and rechecked their data. But the results always came out the same.

Being scientists, not politicians, they prepared to publish their study this past January, come what may. Not so fast! commanded the now-Bush Justice Department. We have a few questions for you. And the Bush DOJ, manned by the same attorneys who had so eagerly snapped up the laughable New Jersey racial profiling report in 1999, proceeded to pelt the speeding researchers with a series of increasingly desperate objections.

The elegant study, designed by the Public Service Research Institute in Maryland, had taken photos with high-speed camera equipment and a radar gun of nearly forty thousand drivers on the turnpike. The researchers then showed the photos to a team of three evaluators who identified the race of the driver. The evaluators had no idea if the drivers in the photos had been speeding. The photos were then correlated with speeds.

The driver identifications are not reliable! whined the Justice Department. The researchers had established a driver's race by agreement among two of the three evaluators. So in response to DOJ's complaint, the researchers reran their analysis, using only photos about which the evaluators had reached unanimous agreement. The speeding ratios came out identically to before.

The data are incomplete! shouted the Justice Department next. About one-third of the photos had been unreadable, because of windshield glare that interfered with the camera, or the driver's position. Aha! said the federal attorneys. Those unused photos would change your results! But that is a strained argument. The only way that the twelve thousand or so unreadable photos would change the study's results would be if windshield glare or a seating position that obstructed the camera disproportionately affected one racial group. Clearly they do not.

Nevertheless DOJ tried to block the release of the report until its objections were answered. "Based on the questions we have identified, it may well be that the results reported in the draft report are wrong or unreliable," portentously wrote Mark Posner, a Justice Department lawyer held over from the Clinton era.

DOJ's newfound zeal for pseudo-scientific nitpicking is remarkable, given its laissez-faire attitude toward earlier slovenly reports that purported to show racial profiling. Where it gets its new social-science expertise is also a mystery, since according to North Carolina criminologist Matthew Zingraff, "there's not a DOJ attorney who knows a thing about statistical methods and analysis." Equally surprising is Justice's sudden unhappiness with the Public Service Research Institute, since it approved the selection of the institute for an earlier demographic study of the turnpike.

The institute proposed a solution to the impasse: Let us submit the study to a peer-reviewed journal or a neutral body like the National Academy of Sciences. If a panel of our scientific peers determines the research to be sound, release the study. No go, said the Justice Department. That study ain't seeing the light of day.

Robert Voas, the study's co-author, is amazed by Justice's intransigence. "I think it's very unfortunate that the politics have gotten in the way of science," he says, choosing his words carefully. "The scientific system has not been allowed to move as it should have in this situation."

As DOJ and the New Jersey attorney general stalled, the *Record* of Bergen County posted the report on the Internet, forcing the state attorney general to release it officially. Now the damage control begins in earnest. Everyone with a stake in the racial profiling myth, from the state attorney general to the ACLU to defense attorneys who have been getting drug dealers out of jail and back on the streets by charging police racism, is trying to minimize the significance of the findings. But they are fighting a rearguard battle. Waiting in the wings are other racial profiling studies by statisticians who actually understand the benchmark problem: Matthew Zingraff's pioneering traffic research in North Carolina, due out soon, as well as sound studies in Pennsylvania, New York, and Miami. Expect many of the results to support the turnpike data, since circumstantial evidence from traffic fatalities and drunk-driving tests have long suggested different driving behaviors among different racial groups. While racist cops undoubtedly do exist—and undoubtedly they are responsible for isolated instances of racial profiling—the evidence shows that systematic racial profiling by police does not exist.

The Bush administration, however desperate to earn racial sensitivity points, should realize that far more than politics is at stake in the poisonous anti–racial profiling agenda. It has strained police-community relations and made it more difficult for the police to protect law-abiding citizens in inner-city neighborhoods. The sooner the truth about policing gets out, the more lives will be saved, and the more communities will be allowed to flourish freed from the yoke of crime.

2002

Diallo Truth,
Diallo Falsehood

JUST AFTER MIDNIGHT on February 4, 1999, four New York City cops took forty-one shots at an unarmed street peddler named Amadou Diallo and plunged the mayoralty of Rudolph Giuliani into crisis. Within a day, a powerful morality tale gripped the city and clung there for the next three months. It ran as follows: "The shooting of Amadou Diallo exposes the dark underbelly of Mayor Giuliani's world-famous crime rout: a culture of police abuse that has struck universal fear into blacks and Hispanics and is now erupting into a broad-based multi-racial protest movement."

Almost nothing in this tale was true. Residents of the city's most crime-ridden neighborhoods are far more positive about the police than the press ever hinted. Empirical data show a police department more cautious with the use of force than at any time in recent history. And the obsessively covered protest movement consisted only of long-standing Giuliani foes, whose importance shriveled when the TV cameras decamped.

The Diallo crisis was a manufactured one—an unparalleled example of the power of the press, and, above all, the *New York Times*, to create the reality it reports. Some people have good reason to resent the police; many more—especially minority New Yorkers—resent them precisely because of the false charges made

35

by activists and echoed incessantly by the press. That's why it's critical to rebut the press's mendacious morality tale from the ground up.

The event that sparked the crisis was horrific. As February 4 began, an unmarked car carrying four undercover police officers from the elite Street Crime Unit cruised down Wheeler Avenue in the Soundview section of the Bronx. Under the Giuliani administration, Street Crime officers aggressively seek out illegal guns—dangerous work, but a key cause of the city's breathtaking 75 percent drop in gun homicides since 1993.

The four cops would have been briefed that night about a rash of shootings in the neighborhood, including the murder of a livery cabdriver. The unit was also looking for an armed rapist responsible for up to fifty-one assaults, including ten in the Soundview section, where he probably lived. The four officers have yet to disclose publicly what happened next; the following speculative account, compiled primarily by the *New York Post*'s crime reporter, rests on sources close to the case.

The cops spotted a slender man pacing nervously in the doorway and peering into the windows of 1157 Wheeler, a small brick apartment building. Officers Sean Carroll and Edward McMellon got out of the car, identified themselves as police, and asked the man to stop. Instead, twenty-two-year-old Amadou Diallo, a peddler of bootlegged videos and tube socks on Manhattan's East 14th Street, continued into the vestibule and tried to get inside the building's inner door. Diallo had recently filed a wildly false application for political asylum, claiming to be a Mauritanian victim of torture orphaned by government security forces. In fact he was a Guinean with two well-off and living parents. He had reason, therefore, not to welcome encounters with authorities.

The two cops ordered Diallo to come out and show them his hands. Turning away, he reached into his pocket and pulled out what Carroll thought was a gun. "Gun!" Carroll shouted. "He's got a gun!" McMellon, who'd followed Diallo up the stairs, feared he was in point-blank danger and shot at Diallo three times before stepping backward, falling off the steps, and breaking his tailbone. Carroll, seeing McMellon down and thinking he'd been shot, opened fire.

As bullets ricocheted into the street, the other two cops concluded that a firefight was under way. They jumped out of the car and began shooting at the figure crouched in the vestibule. Diallo hadn't fallen prone, according to the cops' lawyers, because the 9 mm copper-jacketed bullets passed through him cleanly without bringing him down.

When the shooting stopped, eight to ten seconds later, the officers had fired a total of forty-one rounds, nineteen of which had hit Diallo, perforating his aorta, spinal cord, lungs, and other organs. Two of the officers had emptied their sixteen-bullet magazines. When they searched Diallo's body to retrieve his gun, they found only a black wallet and a shattered beeper in a pool of blood. Officer Carroll wept.

The killing of Amadou Diallo was an unmitigated tragedy, demanding close investigation into police training procedures to see if any feasible safeguards could have prevented it. But nothing in the police department's recent history suggests that it was part of a pattern of excessive force. Nothing that is known of the case to date suggests that the shooting was anything but a tragic mistake; the officers acted in the good-faith, though horribly mistaken, belief that they were under deadly threat. "The majority of officers, because they're not in combat often, feel extreme fear," explains Robert Gallagher, a former Street Crime Unit officer and one of the most decorated detectives in history. "They saw Diallo acting suspiciously, and if one officer says 'gun,' the rest will believe him. In the exchange of gunfire, nothing in your mind says: 'I want to kill this man.'"

Every available fact about the New York Police Department shows how atypical the Diallo shooting was. After three years of steady decline, the cops' use of deadly force was far lower in 1998 than in 1993, the final year of Mayor David Dinkins's administration, currently hailed as a paradigm of peace. In 1998 fewer than 1 percent of the department used their weapons, 25 percent below the 1993 number. Shootings per officer dropped 67 percent from 1993 to 1998. Most impressively, even as police interaction with criminals has risen precipitously since the Dinkins administration, and even as the department has grown by 36 percent, both the absolute number of police killings and the rate of fatalities per officer has fallen. In 1993 the police made 266,313 arrests and killed 23 people, compared with 1998's 403,659 arrests and 19 people killed. In 1990, one year into the allegedly golden Dinkins era, there were two and a half times more fatal shootings per officer than now, while, of course, New Yorkers were being murdered by civilians in record numbers.

Today's NYPD also looks restrained compared with the cops in other cities. In 1998 New York's fatal police shooting rate was 0.48 fatal shootings per 1,000 cops, compared with Philadelphia's 0.72, Miami's 2.01, and Washington, D.C.'s whopping 3.12. Washington's trigger-happy and predominantly black cops fire their weapons seven times more often than New York's, thus belying the endlessly repeated claim that a racially representative force is a more restrained force.

Though the absolute number of civilian complaints rose between 1994 and 1996—concurrently with a growth in the force and greater outreach by the Civilian Complaint Review Board—the rate of civilian complaints per officer dropped by 20 percent. And over the last two years the absolute number of complaints has declined as well, following Commissioner Howard Safir's introduction of civilian complaints into the NYPD's celebrated Compstat (computerized crime analysis) system.

From the day he took office, Rudy Giuliani threatened the foundations of the liberal worldview—denouncing identity politics, demanding work from welfare recipients, and, above all, successfully fighting crime by fighting criminals rather than blathering about crime's supposed "root causes," racism and poverty. It was a godsend for his opponents that the four officers who killed Diallo were white, allowing the incident to stand as proof of alleged departmental racism, the "dark side" (in the *Economist's* triumphant headline) of Giuliani's conquest of crime. Now it was payback time.

The Clinton administration jumped in immediately, sending FBI agents and federal prosecutors to the Bronx to help the local district attorney investigate the shooting and probably to start building a federal case against the officers and the department as well. The president denounced police misconduct (implying that the Diallo officers were guilty of deliberate brutality or racism); Hillary Clinton, readying her New York Senate run, let it be known that she was consulting with local Democratic pols about the Diallo case. Both the U.S. Civil Rights Commission and the Justice Department announced investigations into the NYPD as a whole and the Street Crime Unit in particular; the Justice Department inquiry could ultimately—and preposterously—lead to damaging federal monitoring of the city's police. The state attorney general started his own duplicative inquiry into the department's stop-and-frisk practices. One Police Plaza has become a round-the-clock paperwork-processing center for the numerous investigations.

Meanwhile Al Sharpton and other local activists were experimenting with various protest venues. Sharpton's fellow reverend, Calvin Butts, announced a consumer boycott, whose relevance remained inscrutable. The Reverend Al finally settled on having his followers arrested for sitting in on police headquarters. His big break came when David Dinkins and Congressman Charles Rangel joined his protest and got their picture on the front page of the *New York Times* in plastic handcuffs. Bingo! The civil disobedience campaign became an overnight sensation.

A wider range of Giuliani antagonists—and a very occasional, much-cherished "celebrity," such as Susan Sarandon—started showing up to be photographed and arrested. Not one objected to the vicious anti-police and anti-Giuliani rhetoric spewed out daily by Sharpton followers, nor did any shrink from linking arms with the city's most noisome racial troublemaker, despite his recent conviction for slander in the notorious Tawana Brawley hoax. After the announcement of almost unprecedentedly severe second-degree murder indictments of the four officers, Sharpton and a coalition of left-wing labor leaders and Democratic activists organized a march across the Brooklyn Bridge on April 15 to promote a hastily devised "Ten Point Plan" for police reform.

The more Mayor Giuliani struggled against the net that ensnared him, the more entangled he became. When he burst out in impatience against the media's infatuation with the plastic handcuff charade, his opponents happily denounced his alleged racial insensitivity. His repeated refusals to condemn the entire police department and his insistence on responding to emotion with fact earned him censure for rigidity.

No press organ covered all this more obsessively (with the exception of local news channel New York One) than the *New York Times*. No mere observer of the unfolding events, the *Times* was a major player, enveloping the city in an inescapable web of anti-police Diallo coverage. In the first two months after the shooting, it ran a remarkable 3.5 articles a day on the case, climaxing on March 26—at the height of the Police Plaza protests and when news of the second-degree murder indictment was leaked—with a whopping nine stories. The paper buffed up Al Sharpton and glorified his protest movement. It covered Diallo's burial with loving detail and sentimental drama worthy of Princess Di. Most important, the *Times* created a wholly misleading portrait of a city under siege—not by criminals but by the police. In so doing, it exacerbated the police-minority tensions it purported merely to describe.

The unquestioned assumption of the *Times* coverage, as well as of the protests and government investigations, was that the Diallo shooting was a glaring example of pervasive police misconduct. But since in no way could the Diallo facts—the shooting of a peaceful, unarmed citizen—be shown to be typical of the department, the *Times* zeroed in on a different angle. The Street Crime Unit, and the NYPD generally, it claimed, were using the stop-and-frisk technique to harass minorities. The logic seemed to be that the same racist mentality that leads to unwarranted stop-and-frisks led the four officers to shoot Diallo.

The day after the shooting, the *Times* announced its theme: "Elite Force Quells Crime, But at a Cost, Critics Say." Ten days later the front page put it more bluntly: "Success of Elite Police Force Unit Exacts a Toll on the Streets." Four days after that, another front-page article declared: "After the Shooting, an Eroding Trust in the Police" (big surprise, given the paper's nonstop allegations of widespread police brutality); an op-ed article the same day by a lawyer who makes his living suing the police reiterated: "Dazzling Crime Statistics Come at a Price." Two days later a front-page article in the Sunday Week in Review announced: "Behind Police Brutality, Public Assent." A later article was headlined: "In Two Minority Neighborhoods, Residents See a Pattern of Hostile Street Searches." The burden of the series was that the Street Crime Unit stops minorities for "no reason," creating terrible fear and resentment in the streets. Uproariously, the paper even suggested that African immigrants are in greater danger from New York police than from the security forces of their homelands.

Unquestionably the police under Mayor Giuliani have been using their stop-and-frisk power more aggressively than the Supreme Court opinion establishing the power contemplated. That's true of police departments across the country, though. Unquestionably, too, an active use of stop-and-frisk risks alienating people, especially since many officers fail to show appropriate courtesy when no gun is found. That hardly means, however, that the police are stopping people at random.

The *Times's* own evidence shows something very far from randomness. The Street Crime Unit, the paper says, reported 45,000 frisks in the last two years and made 9,500 arrests, of which 2,500 were for illegal guns. That ratio—one arrest for every 4.7 stops; one gun for every 18 stops—looks pretty impressive, though admittedly the police may not be reporting all stops. Argues Columbia law professor Richard Uviller: "I don't know of any other way to fight the war on handguns—the number-one crime problem in the U.S. today. A system that hits one in 20 is well within tolerance," he maintains. "The ordinary stop-and-frisk is a minimal intrusion."

But to the *Times*, any unsuccessful frisks may be too many. Its gut feeling about the stop-and-frisk issue shone out clearly from a shocked statement in the February 15 "Toll on the Streets" article: "Nearly 40,000 people were stopped and frisked during the last two years *simply because* a street crime officer mistakenly thought they were carrying guns" [emphasis added]. Why else would the police stop and frisk someone? Can the *Times* think the police should stop and frisk only people who actually have guns—an impossible requirement?

Missing from the *Times's* "simply because" conception is any sense of the danger that illegal guns pose or any recollection of the pre-Giuliani reality, when homicides topped 2,200 a year, compared with 633 in 1998. Richard Green, the leader of the Crown Heights Youth Collective, has not forgotten. "I've been to six young people's funerals since January," he says. "If the Street Crime Unit pats me down because I match a description, and the next guy they pat down has a gun, God bless them. I have a right to privacy, but you have an absolute right to your life and property."

The *Times's* coverage of police-community relations had no space for leaders like the dreadlocked Green. Instead, the paper conferred glowing profiles on Lieutenant Eric Adams, a strident internal critic of the police; cartoonist Art Spiegelman, who produced a disgraceful *New Yorker* cover drawing of a jolly policeman aiming at citizen-shaped targets at a shooting gallery; and David Dinkins and Charles Rangel, who competed for the most extreme insults they could hurl at Mayor Giuliani and his crime-fighting record.

Green has no tolerance for lawless police activity, but he has quite a different perspective on the NYPD's efforts to get illegal guns off the street from anything the *Times* reflected. He recalls a young man shot to death in April inside a Brooklyn movie theater. "If I have to choose between the bad and the intolerable," he says, "I'll take the bad. The intolerable is the mother crying in front of the casket, the father telling me: 'You know, the emergency room tried really hard to save his life.' If the mayor is doing something to stop this, God bless him." Green dismisses the image of the Street Crime Unit as rogue cops itching for a fight. "Those guys are not coming from the Yankee game to beat up some guy. When the SCU comes to a community, they're not there randomly. They're there because a Compstat analysis showed high crime in the neighborhood."

Many minority officers echo Green's observation. Mubarak Abdul-Jabbar, now a transit coordinator for the police union, came up to the Bronx courthouse one windy morning in March to support the Diallo officers. Are the police targeting minorities? I ask him. "That's a hard question," Abdul-Jabbar says slowly. "Unfortunately, there's a high rate of crime in black and Latino communities. The Street Crime Unit doesn't go where there's crime per se, but where there's high crime. If there were high rates of crime in Bay Ridge, they'd be there. No one wants to admit the facts," he adds, "that in black and Latino communities, senior citizens have to stay inside." But are the police stopping too many people? "I don't think the police stop and frisk too much," muses Abdul-Jabbar. "The reality is, you have to stop and frisk; no one will announce to you that they have a gun."

Some officers undoubtedly make unjustified stops, but the *Times* rarely bothered to get the police's side of the story (a February 11 article on the dilemma of deciding whether to use one's gun, and a sensible June 20 Sunday magazine article on the controversy over racial profiling were the exceptions). In early May the bulletin board at the Street Crime Unit headquarters notified officers of the following series of armed robberies in the Bronx:

4/22/99 Blue Toyota 5 MB [male blacks] NFD [no further description]
4/23/99 Blue Toyota Uzi and .45 rev. 3 MB NFD
1 FB [female black] NFD
4/28/99 Blue Toyota MB 27, 5'6", 210 lbs.

These descriptions will be just the starting point for further observation and crime-pattern analysis. A broad-chested Street Crime Unit member from a family of police officers explains some possible additional guides. "We're trained to look for things that don't make sense," he says: "people congregating, turning away fast, or holding or picking up their belts, like an off-duty police officer with a gun." Even so, officers searching for the Toyota robbers may well stop some innocent drivers. Which is worse—stopping four innocent people on the basis of reasonable suspicion to make one arrest, or not making the arrest at all?

A preliminary analysis of stop-and-frisk records in more than twenty precincts last year disproves the charge that the police single out minorities for investigation. In fact police frisk blacks at a lower rate than their representation in IDs by crime victims. Victims identified 71 percent of their assailants as black, but only 63 percent of all people frisked were black (and only 68 percent of all arrestees were black). Since the majority of crime is committed by minorities against minorities, inevitably the subjects of frisks will be minorities too.

In talking to city residents about the police, the *Times* found only resentment and suspicion. An article on March 21 on the Model Block program contained a characteristic touch. The paper had triumphantly discovered one of the city's few neighborhoods to turn down the program, in which police cordon off and intensively patrol a street to keep drug dealers from returning. Noting that some residents doubted whether they could reduce crime and drug dealing on their own, the article quickly added: "These residents are not police boosters, . . . but they like drug dealers even less." Phew, we might have thought they actually supported the police! The *Times* noted that these non–police boosters were worried "over well-publicized reports of brutality against . . . minority groups." It did not stop to consider whether that publicity—its own reporting, in other words—was creating the fear it described.

Undeniably the sentiment the *Times* reported is real, and dangerous to the city's social fabric. It also long predates the Giuliani administration. Through much of the nineteenth century, police would enter the Five Points area of lower Manhattan—the city's most noisome Irish slum, with a homicide a night for fifteen years—only in pairs, since they were so hated.

But though this animus toward the police still exists, it is accompanied by goodwill in the very communities where the animus is thickest. "I think the community loves the police; the silent majority is happy," says Street Crime Unit captain Harold Kohlmann, and most cops would agree. Had the *Times* visited a Model Block program one street away from where Diallo was shot, it would have found support for Kohlmann's claim. One April afternoon, Dave Rivera was basking in the bright sun and smoking a cigarette on Elder Avenue, drug-infested until recently. Rivera has lived on the block for twenty-five years and works as superintendent in the building across the street. The Model Block program? "Everybody loves it," he says in heavily accented English. "It's good they're here." Having lived under a drug fiefdom, Rivera offers a street's-eye view of what the police are up against: "Sometimes the police have to be a little rough, they have to play the game. If you be too nice. . . ." He shrugs meaningfully.

Across the street a slender twenty-two-year-old with sunken cheeks and a red bandana around his head is leaning against a chain-link fence. Antonio Espinosa, a carpenter's aide, looks like a prime target for police harassment, but somehow the cops have missed him. "I've never had a problem with the police," he says in Spanish. "I believe if you do right, you won't have a problem."

Many people will find this law-and-order view naive. But naive or not, it has many proponents among minorities. Mario has come to a community meeting at the 43rd Precinct, where the Diallo shooting occurred, to ask the police to clean up a drug problem in his neighborhood. Does he think the police harass people? "Sometimes you're in the wrong place at the wrong time, and people think you targeted them. I'm pretty sure that if you were home where you were supposed to be, nothing would happen to you." The city's recently retired chief of police, Louis Anemone, one of the most revered members of the department and a major catalyst in the Giuliani crime revolution, concurs: "Guys out there at 1 and 2 a.m., stopped on street corners—they're not your average Joe Citizen."

A constant *Times* theme was that people had "exchange[d] the fear of crime for a fear of the police," as an April 2 editorial solemnly charged. Some people, mysteriously, haven't picked up that terror. Asked if she feared the police, Freddie, a middle-aged woman attending the 43rd Precinct's May community council meeting, unhesitatingly answers no. Are the police racist? "I don't feel they're racist. We have very good officers." Pointing to her grandson and foster daughter, she says: "These two children, I try to teach them the police is their friend. When they come into the neighborhood, we talk, so they know they are there to help them."

This view has advocates even on Wheeler Avenue, where Amadou Diallo was shot. Pushing a cart filled with laundry one day last April, a few houses down from Diallo's former apartment, a boy named Eric says: "The police are here to protect us from bad guys and to stop the drug dealers. Before, parents couldn't let their kids out." Eric is no Pollyanna, however. "Some police are bad guys," he adds judiciously. "They don't know how to react against other people."

It turns out the *Times* had to work pretty hard to avoid people like this. A recent Justice Department study found that 77 percent of New York City blacks approve of the police, an astoundingly high number, considering the relentless anti-police propaganda of activists and the press. The *Times* tried desperately to neutralize this refutation of its own coverage by playing up the paltry 12 percent gap between black and white approval ratings.

On the street it's not difficult to find a more nuanced view of police-citizen interactions than the *Times's* simple aggressor-victim model. Sharit Sherrod, a twenty-three-year-old inventory specialist, is standing in line at the 43rd Precinct to report a stolen car. He's had friends who've been arrested, he says—not surprisingly, since he has many friends in the Bloods. "But I don't run into the same problems with the police as the average black man," he explains, "because I know how to talk to them. I don't get an attitude, I don't take it personally. A lot of my friends start cursing, but the way I look at it, the cops carry guns."

Sherrod is on to something. While there is no justification for the police treating peaceful citizens hostilely or rudely, police-citizen relations are a two-way street. Two 1998 studies for the National Institute of Justice found that citizens are more inclined to show the police disrespect than vice versa, and that the most powerful predictor of police disrespect is a citizen being disrespectful first. The nonstop coverage of the Diallo shooting has already increased the taunts thrown at the police on the street, escalating tensions.

No claim of police harassment seemed incredible to the *Times.* A troubling article told of police harassment of students at Rice High School, a Catholic school; one boy alleged that an officer had accused him of personally knitting the school sweater vest he was wearing in order to pass as a student. Perhaps every teen regaling reporters with his police ordeals tells only the gospel truth, but on the streets you hear skepticism about such accounts. "I'm sure the students provoke the police," sighs Lilliam Rosa, the youth coordinator for the Highbridge Unity Center in the South Bronx.

"It's the attitude of kids these days: no respect for the police or other adults." Rosa's students are nearly all from Catholic schools; in her youth group they tell of "looking hard" at the police, whom, she says, they hate. "Then they say: 'What you looking at?' and it makes the police suspicious." The cops have stopped some boys in her group at night to check their backpacks for guns—not a bad policy, she thinks. "The police just check them, then let them go," she says, "but most people react. Then the police react."

John Vargas, a hospital financial investigator and president of the community council in the 43rd Precinct, greets many police-harassment stories with similar skepticism. "I say: 'Tell me what you did, not just what the cops did.' People won't honestly admit they did something wrong to provoke the police. People will always say this and that, but when you ask for concrete information, they walk away." The fact that only 5 percent of the complaints filed before the Civilian Complaint Review Board are ever substantiated, with many dismissed for failure to follow up, supports such skepticism.

A recent claimant to police-victim status shows how tenuous such claims can be. At Sharpton's April 15 march across the Brooklyn Bridge, a woman in the high-profile row of police-brutality victims was carrying a photograph of her bruised and cut son, Jovan Gonzalez. It turns out the police never laid a finger on Jovan. But the "racist gang" who did beat him up has "ties," Ms. Gonzalez claimed, to the 47th Precinct. Gonzalez has already entered popular lore as a police victim; no one has ever asked for proof of the involvement of the 47th Precinct.

Like liberal critics of the police throughout the city, the *Times* was shocked, shocked by the Street Crime Unit's motto: "We Own the Night." Here was proof of the marauding attitude of this renegade outfit! The *Times* neglected to report that the motto frames a silhouette of an old lady bent over a cane; the unit proudly asserts supremacy over thugs it unapologetically views as evil, in order to protect the helpless.

Fearless of self-contradiction, the *Times* played up the claim that racism causes the police to ignore crime against ghetto residents, even as it trumpeted claims that the police were too aggressive in trying to get guns out of the ghetto. A February 17 article quoted minority women who complained that the police were ignoring the serial rapist terrorizing the Bronx and upper Manhattan. If a white woman is attacked, the police are all over the case, complained a West Harlem community advocate, but "when we have fifteen-year-old girls beaten and raped, nobody comes to do anything." A Washington Heights woman bathetically doubted that the police would catch the rapist: "We are Spanish people, poor people. They might care if this was the Upper West Side."

Though in former days the police did ignore ghetto crime, today Compstat's crime analysis does not give extra points to white neighborhoods but targets crime wherever it occurs. The Street Crime Unit had gone to the 43rd Precinct precisely to track down the rapist; had the rapist not been out there, Diallo probably would still be alive. Were there angry demonstrations against the rape suspect when, after clever sleuthing, the police finally arrested him not too far from Wheeler Avenue? Of course not.

So overwhelming was the case against the police, in the *Times*'s view, that Giuliani's unaccountable support for them was front-page news. "Giuliani Softens His Tone But Still Defends the Police," the paper reported incredulously on March 24. Instead of reporting the numerous positive data on the police, the *Times* left the task to Giuliani and then implied that his was an advocacy position rather than a statement of statistical fact. "While Giuliani has expressed sympathy and concern over the shooting, he continued to deny a pattern of excessive force in the department," marveled the paper on February 10. But Giuliani "continued to deny" such a pattern because none existed, as the *Times* itself could easily have ascertained.

The nonstop Diallo coverage had its desired effect. A March 16 front-page article smacked its lips at the plunge in Giuliani's approval ratings from 63 percent to 42 percent and announced that "many think police are biased." No wonder. Since the dark days of Giuliani's high ratings, noted the *Times*, "one issue has overshadowed all others, the death of Amadou Diallo." But it was a deliberate editorial decision, not an imperative of nature, that made that issue predominate. As Giuliani observed, if the press had been covering a recent murder of a guest at the Waldorf Astoria with the same obsession as the Diallo shooting, everyone would be convinced there was a growing murder problem in New York, even though murders were down 70 percent.

While embroidering its theme of the out-of-control police, the *Times* ran increasingly starry-eyed stories on the protest movement. At first the paper occasionally noted the demonstrators' advocacy of violence, along with the death threats and obscenities they hurled at the police. But a different theme soon dominated: the heartwarming and progressive diversity of the protesters and the ever-increasing stature and statesmanship of the Reverend Al Sharpton.

In its relentless diversity coverage, the *Times* simply echoed the organizers' line. "In every photo and every event, there would be some sense of a rainbow," former Dinkins aide Ken Sunshine told the *New York Observer*. "If we had to drag someone in at the last minute to complete the photo, then we would do it." The *Times* was only too happy to be spun.

But then, in a cute postmodern twist, the *Times* acknowledged its own spun state and the made-for-the-media nature of the protests. "The carefully scripted parade has drawn unflagging press coverage," reporter Dan Barry confided in an extraordinary March 19 front-page article, with the most extraordinary front-page headline of the whole affair: "Daily Protesters in Handcuffs Keep Focus on Diallo Killing." Here was a completely self-referential piece posing as news: the paper covering itself covering the Diallo protests. The article might as well have been headlined: "We Keep

Focus on Diallo Killing." Further signaling his postmodern aware-
ness of the media game, Barry commented on the staged nature of
the events: four of the day's prominent black arrestees, he wrote,
"made a striking image for the scrum of news photographers."

If anything, Barry understated how completely media-driven
the civil disobedience campaign was. As I chatted with a Sharpton
follower one morning at One Police Plaza, a woman in a sleek suit
paced nearby, casting impatient glances at me. Finally I asked her
what she wanted. State Assemblymen Richard Gottfried and Pete
Grannis were getting arrested that day, she portentously announced, then disappeared to spread the word among other reporters.

The ratio of cameras and reporters to protesters on the plaza
easily approached one-to-one. Commissioner Safir needn't have
made his ill-timed trip to the Oscars; he could have imbibed the
same air of media-fabulousness outside his own workplace. The un-
reality rivaled any Hollywood production: here were Sharpton attorney Michael Hardy and Giuliani-basher Norm Siegel of the
NYCLU backslapping and sharing jokes with top police brass,
while the "NYPD = KKK" signs bobbed nearby. Here were the allegedly brutal officers politely informing people where they should
go to get arrested.

An eager swarm of reporters encircled Sharpton upon his arrival each day, climbing over one another like drones trying to get
to the queen bee. Then the day's high-profile arrestees would link
arms with the Reverend, about fifty yards from the entrance to police headquarters, and wait patiently for the signal while Sharpton
stared wordlessly at the building with a noble faraway look, like
Telemachus faithfully scanning the horizon for the long-vanished
Odysseus. Finally the glorious march would begin, past the rows of
cameras, down the brick walk to the revolving glass doors, and
Sharpton would hand his current batch of arrestees off to the police like an usher presenting guests to a receiving line. Some high-

profile arrestees found ways to make the moment even more meaningful: the *Times* noted reverently that Susan Sarandon "walked to her arrest singing 'We Shall Overcome' quietly."

Meanwhile the *Times* tried out a little historical revisionism regarding the early protests. A March 26 article recalled that the protests were "small and sporadic at first, quiet prayer vigils or subdued marches involving only a few dozen supporters of the Diallo family." Quiet prayer vigils? How about the warning issued by the viciously racist Khalid Abdul Muhammad at the February 12 homegoing service for Diallo: "You shoot one of ours 41 times, we shoot 41 of yours one time. One shot, one kill." And the paper stopped listening to the regulars who showed up every day to wave banners at One Police Plaza—people like the man who yelled at officers that he'd kill them, or like Carol Taylor, a Sharpton groupie in a yellow African hat, who every day screamed hoarsely at the nearest cop: "P.U., I smell something blue!"

So the *Times* never noticed that the "rainbow" message that Ken Sunshine and other organizers worked so assiduously to convey didn't trickle down to the troops. When two Sharpton followers learned that one pro-police demonstrator, Gloria Horsham, had a white son-in-law, they could not contain their contempt for the sixty-seven-year-old Trinidadian. "You're filled with self-hate, so you taught your children to go after Caucasians," sneered a middle-aged woman from New Jersey. "Go back to Trinidad; don't bring that stuff here!" An older man, unfazed by Horsham's retort that if she is so filled with self-hate, how come her other children had married blacks, chuckled condescendingly: "You want to bleach yourself out." Bill Lord, a former Sharpton campaign manager, hadn't gotten that rainbow feeling, either. He coolly told me that while I couldn't understand him, he could understand me. "I'm a specialist on white people," he assured me, "because they're the deceivers."

For all the determined spinning, the protests were hardly integrated. Politically they were monochromatic, ranging from the unions opposing Giuliani's welfare reforms on the right flank to the Young Communist League on the left. The groups that sent members to get arrested at One Police Plaza represent every interest that Giuliani's efforts to dismantle poverty and identity politics have offended, from the NAACP, the National Congress for Puerto Rican Rights, Jews for Racial and Economic Justice, the CUNY faculty, and the National Lawyers Guild to ACT-UP, the Committee Against Anti-Asian Violence, Housing Works, the Center for Constitutional Rights, the War Resisters League, Workers to Free Mumia, the Working Families Party, Lesbians and Gays Against Police Brutality, New York Lawyers in the Public Interest, and various unions. The most strident members of the City Council turned up at One Police Plaza, as did the State Legislature's Black, Puerto Rican, and Hispanic caucus. Few left-wing causes couldn't be piggybacked onto the Diallo episode. A poster outside Sharpton's headquarters denouncing Giuliani's workfare program read: "Shooting people like Amadou Diallo is one way to commit murder, starving people is another!"

Too bad former mayor Ed Koch, who had intended to get arrested with Susan Sarandon, never made it to One Police Plaza. His arrest would have been the icing on the protest movement's hypocrisy. Not that he hadn't gotten in his media licks against Giuliani already, labeling him "nasty" on New York One and admonishing him to start speaking out about "racism" in the NYPD. In the *Times*, he had pontificated that being mayor "requires a willingness to hear. So we're saying to the Mayor: 'Listen.'"

The phrase must have brought a certain feeling of *déjà entendu*, since in 1983, during an episode eerily foreshadowing Giuliani's current problems, a *Times* editorial had commanded then-mayor Koch to "Listen" to complaints of police brutality. Koch had had the temerity to question an account of police harassment then in the news. Such intolerable candor brought the

Feds rushing up from Washington for hearings on police brutality and racism; familiar figures from the Diallo episode included Charles Rangel, Reverend Calvin Butts, and Jesse Jackson.

Koch fought to head off the planned hearings tooth and nail. Look at the facts, he argued with acerbity: the department has a far better record on brutality than elsewhere. It didn't work. "Listen!" admonished the *Times*. Facts are not appropriate; empathy is: "When people rush to pour out their stories," the paper editorialized, "what they want from their leaders is not an argument but an ear." A parade of witnesses launched the identical charges of racism and insensitivity against Koch that Giuliani would face fifteen years later.

Today Koch has come round to the position that, in attacking the police, data don't count. "There's a greater number of corrupt and brutal cops today than ever before," he told me. What does he base his conclusion on? "I talk to people," he said. But don't the data show that police use of force is way down? "You're an advocate," he snapped.

What judgment should we make of current public officials who went to One Police Plaza to get arrested? By blocking police headquarters they implied that the department was illegitimate and so should be prevented from functioning even at the risk of imprisonment—a message both false and irresponsible. If officials such as comptroller Carl McCall, the third-highest elected official in the state, feel that the legal regime they administer should be disabled, they should resign. (McCall declined to be interviewed on his decision to get arrested.)

That so many Democratic politicians so lightly tripped over to One Police Plaza for arrest shows how debased the currency of civil disobedience had become in Sharpton's hands. No pol seriously believed that the NYPD was so unjust that it required civil-rights-style demonstrations to resist it, and no pol expected any penalties—correctly so: there were none. Instead, "arrestees" grumbled over the time spent in booking. A student of Richard

Green's correctly called the charade "designer arrests," noting that real arrests entail sitting in a holding cell for two days, eating bologna sandwiches, and coming home only if you're lucky. Green fumes: "The youth saw the [black] leadership marching in handcuffs; it legitimates being in handcuffs."

For all the hyperbole surrounding the arrests, the final tally—1,166—hardly adds up to overwhelming support for Sharpton's cause. A second test of Sharpton's drawing strength, the April 15 march across the Brooklyn Bridge, came up even shorter, considering the resources behind it. The planners drew on the massive capacity of the health-care workers union, Local 1199, headed by Dennis Rivera, an implacable foe of Giuliani's efforts to privatize the city's dinosaur public hospital system. To recruit marchers, Rivera's state-of-the-art publicity machine printed hundreds of thousands of posters and leaflets; his phone banks made 150,000 calls. The Dinkins administration-in-exile took over the union's media center, with Dinkins's ex-chief of staff, Bill Lynch, directing operations, while former aide Ken Sunshine managed the media. Union media expert Bill Batson gave tours to reporters of the march's command center, around whose huge paper- and takeout-food-covered table political operatives, on loan from various City Council members, planned strategy. Batson, youthful and high-strung, with a chrysanthemum mop of dreadlocks and dental braces, proudly pointed out the operatives' gorgeous diversity: here's the former Black Panther (duly noted by the *Times*); here's the aide to City Council member Christine Quinn, whose recent swearing-in ceremony, attended by David Dinkins and Senator Charles Schumer, featured readings from the lesbian play *The Vagina Monologues*.

The anticipation of a kill was palpable. "A month ago, people were scared to say anything bad about the mayor; now he's being compared to Bull Connor in print," marvels Batson, in his tiny office crammed with posters like "10 Things You Can Do to Free [convicted cop killer] Mumia." Leaning back in his chair, Batson gossips on the phone with Elinor Tatum, editor of the *Amsterdam News*, while carrying on a second conversation. "I want you to know, Ellie, I was grandfather of the ads," Batson boasts, referring to a slanderous anti-police television commercial the union and other funders had just released. "I'm glad those 'Fooliani' pieces [a vituperative anti-Giuliani series in the *Amsterdam News*] started up again," he says. "And that *New York* piece—oh my God!" he crows in delight, referring to a blistering cover story on Giuliani.

The recent TV commercial, portraying two ominously angry white cops and one very terrified black boy, put its sponsors on the defensive. As a portrait of Rigoberta Menchu, the patron saint of political fibbers, looked down from the wall of 1199's reception room, the tightly coiled union boss Dennis Rivera ducked reporters' questions comparing the ad to the Willie Horton commercial. But the little flurry of negative publicity around the ad may have been welcome. The official propaganda—the flyers, the ads—is not the real point, reveals Batson conspiratorially. "The meat of this," he says, "is the free media. We're managing the media consciously, because we have no fucking money"—a plea of penury that's hard to swallow sitting in 1199's gleaming headquarters. The result, in Batson's view, was triumphant: "We have captured the imagination of the city of New York."

If so, most people decided to imagine at home rather than come out to march. Days before, at Sharpton's headquarters, attorney Michael Hardy had envisioned "20,000 to 50,000 people coming across the bridge." In fact, police estimates of the march ranged from 4,500 to 10,000. A media consensus emerged toward the lower number. And a visitor from another planet would have concluded that the protest was a joint effort on behalf of Diallo and cop killer Mumia, so numerous were the "Free Mumia" signs bobbing in the crowd. Once the cameras went home, the movement against police brutality collapsed. Two weeks after the April 15 march, a Sharpton-endorsed anti-police group held a meeting, and seven assorted socialists showed up.

Of all the stories the *Times* wove into its Diallo morality tale, none strained credulity more than the maturing of Al Sharpton. While virtually ignoring his past history of racial slander, the *Times* portrayed Sharpton as having been pushed into the Diallo case only by the appeal of a supporter (Sharpton gave the same story to the *Village Voice* but changed the identity of the supporter). It also presented him as the passive recipient of the Diallo family's appeal for help: never has his "renown and resourcefulness . . . been as clear as this week," marveled the paper, "when a bereaved family from another continent turned to [him] for help."

In fact Sharpton tried desperately from the start to capture the Diallos for his own use. He raged with resentment when he heard that the mayor had reached out to Amadou's parents: "Oh God, what are they trying to do here?" he recalled for the *Village Voice*. Giuliani, of course, was trying to offer his condolences and help, and had he met with the parents, the next three months might have been different. But Sharpton dispatched a brigade to the airport to try to get to the parents before the Giuliani people. To the great detriment of the city, he captured his quarry. The mother rebuffed Giuliani's assistance, and from then on Sharpton used every opportunity to rub the mayor's nose in his defeat and to use the photogenic Mrs. Diallo to advance his cause. He made Giuliani wait for over an hour for the parents on the day of Diallo's funeral and then disclosed that the family would not see him at all. "I hate to blow the mayor's bubble here," Sharpton triumphantly announced, "but they are not preoccupied with the mayor."

A falser statement was never uttered. Sharpton, who scripts what the Diallos are preoccupied with, is obsessed with Giuliani. Ever since the mayor refused to meet with him after an ambush of the police at a Harlem mosque in January 1994, Sharpton has fumed at being denied access. "You've been running from me for the last four years. But now it's me and you, Rudy," he declared after the savage police assault on Abner Louima in 1997, "and I'm going to whip you all over town."

Speaking to supporters at his National Action Headquarters, a large, low-ceilinged room in Harlem with a plaid carpet and large portraits of himself and other black activists on the walls, Sharpton erased any ambiguity about the real political agenda of the Diallo movement. Addressing Giuliani in absentia, he vowed: "All that barking and talking will come back to haunt you. Only God could arrange for this trial right before your run for the Senate," he roared. "I think the mayor needs a long rest and I intend to help give him that. . . . I'm going to march until I march up those steps [of City Hall] and take my seat inside."

If Sharpton ever does reach City Hall, he will get an adoring reception from the City Council members, among the silliest of the Diallo case's anti-police critics. It was a remarkable experience to watch them lecture Commissioner Howard Safir on how to police during an April 19 Public Safety Committee hearing. Stephen Di-Brienza, the council's most histrionic grandstander, bellowed for more community policing and less anti-crime activity. Safir responded acidly: "The time you referred to, when there was allegedly more community policing, there were also 2,240 murders in the city." Amazingly, DiBrienza replied: "I'm not sure of the relevance of that." Shot back Safir: "It's of relevance to the people killed."

Council members spent most of their energy excoriating various breaches of political correctness. Many took wallops at the department's allegedly inadequate diversity. Too bad they didn't witness a one-sided exchange between three black toughs and a young black police officer at the April 15 march, which might have challenged their facile assumptions about police diversity and community relations. "Yo! Fuck you! You want to put a plunger up our ass?" the self-identified "hip-hop producers" spat at the impassive officer.

But nothing produced quite the excitement as an exchange between Councilwoman Ronnie Eldridge and Safir. After announcing imperiously: "Our children are being taught to fear the police," Eldridge threw down the gauntlet: "Is there not a way to keep crime statistics down without violating civil liberties?" Safir would have none of it. "Is that like: 'When did I stop beating my wife?'" he snapped.

Oooh—not just racism, but sexism! Christine Quinn, of *Vagina Monologues* fame, sputtered: "I don't think domestic violence is anything to joke about, Commissioner." And the commissioner's alleged insensitivity to women then became the leitmotif of the rest of the hearing.

Quinn and her colleagues found a perfect partner for their staged distress in Lieutenant Eric Adams, the persistent police critic and head of One Hundred Blacks in Law Enforcement Who Care. Adams signaled his readiness for the game in his opening statement. "I'm appalled that the council allowed the police commissioner to make light of women being beaten," he declared. He had brought along a hooded witness, a former member of the Street Crime Unit, to testify to the unit's brutality and racism. He hustled the witness in and out of the council chamber with great drama, including loud allegations that police spies were in the room. But it later turned out that the former officer, a woman, had an abysmal record on the force, including an assault on a superior, psychological instability, and malingering, and Safir had fired her a week before her anti-police testimony.

It's hard to top such anti-police foolishness, but the U.S. Commission on Civil Rights came close in its May 26 hearing in New York. The exchange between Mayor Giuliani and a row of Sharpton hecklers, led by "P.U., I smell something blue" shouter Carol Taylor, provided an unparalleled duet between rationality and prejudice. Every fact Giuliani presented about the police, the Sharpton devotees met with closed-minded contempt. Do the police now shoot far fewer people than in 1990, even though there are eight thousand more officers? "What's the relevance of that?" Are fatal shootings by the police way down? "Oh, yeah, only blacks." Do FBI statistics show that New York is the safest large city in the country?

"Stop it please, you make me sick!" One supporter shouted out the theme of the entire hearing: "I'm tired of statistics. He doesn't talk about the reality of racism."

Commission chairwoman and longtime practitioner of race politics Mary Frances Berry adopted the David Dinkins method of crowd control: let them vent. While the hecklers were virtually drowning out Giuliani, only once did she ever so delicately tap her gavel, grinning broadly at the Sharptonites. When they interrupted her, however, "BANG!" went the gavel.

With no more interest in the facts than the Sharpton crew, Berry cut off Giuliani's recital of data about the NYPD's low use of force to ask her all-consuming question: "Do you believe the NYPD fairly represents the population of New York City?" Berry should have known how irrelevant the query was. The new chief of her local police force in Washington, D.C., recently begged the Justice Department to investigate it for civil rights violations, even though the force is majority black.

From then on, it was all uninformed second-guessing and attempts to trivialize the Giuliani crime rout. "Isn't it the case that bias crimes, brutality, and allegations of domestic abuse by police officers went up at the same time that crime went down?" she asked portentously. More police insensitivity to women! Not surprisingly, Giuliani did not have the figures on police domestic abuse at his fingertips.

Before dismissing Giuliani, Berry made clear how little of what he had said had made any impression on her. "Some of the choices appear stark, listening to you," she intoned gravely. "We could protect safety by ignoring civil rights protections." Everything Giuliani had said, however, emphasized that the department insisted on improving police respect for citizens even as it fights crime. But Berry made sure that the record reflected the specious claim that Giuliani's crime turnaround had a "dark side," making New York, in effect, a police state. And though Berry couldn't ensure the mayor the courtesy of a respectful hearing, she was all graciousness to another figure in the drama. "I recognize that the Reverend Al Sharpton has already arrived," she beamed. "I just want to acknowledge the work he has been doing"—"work" that consists of keeping race tensions as high as possible.

The Diallo follies have damaged the city enormously. The 23 percent of black New Yorkers who do not approve of the police have grown angrier. Street Crime Unit officers, well aware of the increased hostility toward them, have pulled back: their felony arrests fell 47 percent in the first four months of 1999, compared with 1998. Shootings and gun homicides are ticking up in the neighborhoods where the unit patrols; citywide, murders were 10 percent higher from February 4 to May 23, 1999, compared with the same period of 1998. And needless to say, the four Diallo officers have almost surely lost the chance of a fair trial.

What should we do? Commissioner Safir is right to reject the claim that crime in New York is low enough, so the police should change their mission. Continuing to bring crime down is the best civil rights program he can offer, since blacks make up four times the number of homicide victims as whites, and the streets of minority neighborhoods have until recently been less safe for their law-abiding residents to walk than other parts of the city. Safir is also right to push the cops to show more respect for civilians. Too many officers have a rude, contemptuous attitude, and Safir's excellent, and unfairly maligned, Courtesy, Professionalism, and Respect training program for cops is a good antidote.

But if the police bear a heavy responsibility for maintaining cordial community relations, the community shares that responsibility too. It is a travesty that Sharpton and his eager new followers focus all their energy on stigmatizing the police. If they spent half their lung and media power on stigmatizing criminals, and the other half on helping young people compete in the job market, they could transform the city.

1999

What Really Happened in Cincinnati

IN APRIL 2001, when riots erupted in Cincinnati, the national media let out a glad cry: black rage, that hottest of political commodities, was back!

The subsequent postriot drill, perfected over the last four decades, unfolded without flaw: instant discovery of the riot's "root causes"; halfhearted condemnation of the violence, followed immediately by its enthusiastic embrace as a "wake-up call" to America; warnings of future outbreaks if the "wake-up call" is ignored; and hurried formation of task forces promising rapid aid for Cincinnati's inner city.

"Riot ideology"—historian Fred Siegel's caustic phrase for the belief that black rioting is a justified answer to white racism—is alive and well in twenty-first-century America. Riots may be relatively rare, but the thinking that rationalizes them is not. It pervades the country's response to underclass problems and to race issues generally. The Cincinnati riots and their aftermath offer a peerless example of all that is wrong with this conventional approach to race. But in Cincinnati, too, if you look, are the clearest possible guideposts for how to get race issues right.

A fatal police shooting of an unarmed teenager, Timothy Thomas, triggered the riots. After 2 a.m. on Saturday, April 7,

Thomas spotted two Cincinnati police officers and started running. Wanted on fourteen warrants for traffic offenses and for evading arrest, Thomas led the policemen on a chase through the narrow alleys of Cincinnati's most drug-infested and violent neighborhood, Over-the-Rhine. The area's Italianate walk-ups, home in the late nineteenth century to one of America's most culturally rich and densely populated German-American communities, today often are either abandoned or given over to methadone clinics, drop-in centers, or Section 8 public housing.

Officer Steve Roach, hearing a radio alert about a fleeing suspect with fourteen warrants, joined the pursuit and came abruptly face-to-face with the nineteen-year-old in a dark alley. When Thomas appeared to reach for his waistband, Roach shot him once in the chest. Three days later Over-the-Rhine would be burning.

Cincinnati's riots hardly constituted a spontaneous outcry against injustice. A demagogic campaign against the police, of the kind common in American cities today, had already heated black residents almost to the boiling point. "Thirteen black men!"—a tally of the suspects killed by the Cincinnati police since 1995—was the rallying cry of protesters in the City Council chambers last fall. Thomas's shooting (added to a January shoot-out death) brought the total to fifteen, and black politicians duly updated their cry to "Fifteen black men," in effect charging that Cincinnati's cops were indiscriminately mowing down black citizens. With robotic predictability, every national news account of the riots repeated the cry, to demonstrate Cincinnati's racism.

In fact, the list of the fifteen police victims shows the depraved nature not of Cincinnati's cops but of its criminals. Harvey Price, who heads the roster, axed his girlfriend's fifteen-year-old daughter to death in 1995, then held a SWAT team at bay for four hours with a steak knife, despite being maced and hit with a stun gun. When he lunged at an officer with the knife, the cop shot him. Jermaine Lowe, a parole violator wanted for armed robbery, fled in a stolen car at the sight of a police cruiser, crashed into another car, then unloaded his handgun at the pursuing officers. Alfred Pope robbed, pistol-whipped, and most likely fired at three people in an apartment hallway, just the latest assault by the vicious twenty-three-year-old, who had already racked up eighteen felony charges and five convictions. He then aimed his handgun at close range at the pursuing officers, and they shot him dead in return.

To call such lowlifes martyrs to police brutality is a stretch. Besides the Thomas shooting, only three of the fifteen cases raise serious questions about officer misjudgment and excessive force. The notion that race was the controlling element in the fifteen deaths is even more absurd.

But it is perfectly in keeping with Cincinnati's racialized politics. Advocates of the city's status quo, whether opposing competitive bidding for city services or blocking the investigation of low-income housing fraud, can bring the City Council to its knees by playing the race card. For the last two years, black nationalists calling themselves the Special Forces have turned up regularly in the delicately carved council chambers of Cincinnati's Romanesque City Hall to spew anti-white and anti-Semitic diatribes. Two days after the Thomas shooting, on Monday, April 9, they were back, accompanied by hundreds of angry black residents, by Timothy Thomas's mother, and by her attorney Kenneth Lawson—Cincinnati's answer to Johnnie Cochran.

The Council meeting instantly spun out of control. Backed by constant screaming from the crowd, lawyer Lawson and another racial activist, the Reverend Damon Lynch III, masterfully inflamed the crowd's anger by suggesting that city officials were willfully withholding information about the Thomas shooting. Lawson, and doubtless Lynch too, knew full well that disclosing Officer Roach's testimony after the shooting would jeopardize the investigation and possible prosecution of the case, yet both threatened to hold every chamber occupant hostage until Roach's testimony was released. Some of the Council Democrats seconded the threats. Three chaotic hours later, Lawson and Lynch grudgingly agreed to disband, Lynch demanding that the police chief "call off the dogs [i.e., officers] outside."

The crowd left City Hall and, swelling to more than one thousand along the way, headed toward the boxy, low-slung police headquarters. Protesters screamed at the officers protecting the station and snapped photos of them, promising lethal revenge for the fifteen black "murders." Someone threw a rock that shattered the station's front door; others pulled the flag from its pole and hung it upside down; police horses were hit; officers were injured by flying glass—but the order was: "Let them vent." The lieutenant in charge even gave a protester a bullhorn in the hope of calming the crowd. It didn't work.

Finally, at 1 a.m., police started arresting those who were hurling rocks and bottles at the station house. Too late: the violence had begun. Over the next three days, crowds would rampage through Cincinnati's poorest neighborhoods, beating white motorists, burning property, breaking hundreds of store windows, and making off with the appliances, furniture, clothing, and booze within. Gunmen fired thousands of shots, many at officers. The police chief begged black clergy for help in restoring calm but got little response.

Though the police were outmatched and overworked, Democratic mayor Charles Luken refused to take additional measures against the violence. Then on Thursday, a bullet hit a cop, grazing off his belt buckle. That afternoon, Luken imposed an 8 p.m. curfew and announced a state of emergency.

By then the riot ideologues were in full cry. The NAACP's Kweisi Mfume flew in to declare Cincinnati the "belly of the whale" of police violence against young black men. Al Sharpton called for federal oversight not just of Cincinnati's but of the nation's police. *Time* magazine named Cincinnati a "model of racial injustice." The *New York Times* found pervasive economic discrimination against the city's blacks. White gentrifiers, pronounced *The New Republic*, lay behind the riots. The *Los Angeles Times* and ABC's *This Week* noted how salutary the violence had been.

Local leaders scrambled to contain the public relations fiasco and to show their concern for black anger. The City Council hurriedly voted to submit a pending racial profiling lawsuit to costly "mediation," rather than contest it, even though none of the suit's allegations had been shown to be credible. Mayor Luken invited in the Justice Department to investigate the police division, which could result in federal oversight of the kind that busts municipal budgets. But the city's main riot response was to form Community Action Now (CAN), a three-man panel dedicated to racial reconciliation through, as its members and promotional materials insist, action, action, and more action. Its three co-chairs are Ross Love, an ex–Procter & Gamble vice president who now heads a black radio empire; Tom Cody, an executive vice president of Federated Department Stores; and the Reverend Damon Lynch, the activist who calls the police "dogs."

At CAN's inception, Ross Love, the official spokesman, announced five task forces to "address the root causes of the recent unrest." The groups, manned by local civil rights figures, business leaders, and poverty advocates, would address "education and youth development, economic inclusion, police and the justice system, housing and neighborhood development, and image and media." But "root causes" have a way of proliferating: soon Love created a sixth task force to look at "health care and human services." And as a harbinger of its future largesse, CAN then hired a former black city manager at $1,400 a day as "special counsel."

With the formation of CAN, and the media agitation that preceded it, we are ready to test the central tenets of riot ideology. In place of "riots," any other element of underclass behavior, such as crime, can be substituted—the rationalizations are identical.

Start with the contention that riots are a response to white racism, since this is the mother of all "root cause" arguments, first popularized by the Kerner Commission Report on the 1960s riots. Ross Love gives this argument an economic spin: racially based "economic exclusion" is his mantra for explaining why blacks rioted in his city. The *New York Times* jumped on the "economic exclusion" bandwagon as well, claiming that Cincinnati has long "frustrated" blacks' justified demands for a "share of prosperity."

To test that hypothesis, walk around Cincinnati's poorest areas, from the river basin, spanned by John A. Roebling's first, beautiful suspension bridge, up to the city's seven surrounding green hills, which in Cincinnati's nineteenth-century heyday compressed its population into a greater density than anywhere but Manhattan. You will see knots of young men in their teens and twenties milling about on almost every street corner, towels draped over their heads, their shorts hanging far below their underwear. Heat has driven some out of their apartments, but many others are there to peddle drugs hidden in crevices in the old brick buildings. I approached a group of boys leaning against a tiny convenience store on a steep intersection called the Five Corners. One boy's T-shirt read: "No Justice, No Peace, These Our Streets, F—k the Police, 1981–2001"—presumably Timothy Thomas's dates. I introduced myself and asked if they'd answer a few questions. "Hell, no!" In a blink of an eye, all but one of the boys had disappeared across the street and into a parking lot or down the steep incline.

Inside the tiny, dark store, a fortyish Jordanian with a mustache and a receding hairline stands squeezed behind the register. He will only give his name as "Mike." "We call the police five to ten times a day," he says quietly. "They drive through and tell them to move." What are they selling? He casts his eyes down. "I don't know; I don't want to talk about it."

At least Mike's store has not been shot at. Under the shredded red awning of Johnnie's Supermarket in the Walnut Hills neighborhood, spider-web cracks radiate across the window from a bullet hole. The bullet's target—a large red sign prohibiting loitering and giving the police the authority to come onto the premises at any time—is still visible under the cracked window. Until recently, up to fifty young men stood in front of Johnnie's, hawking drugs and extorting money from the market's customers. They are mostly gone now, thanks to an undercover operation that netted nineteen indictments. But in front of an abandoned building kitty-corner from Johnnie's, ten young men in white T-shirts shift back and forth.

Now, remember the "economic exclusion" argument: Cincinnati's racist power structure is excluding hordes of qualified young black men. Well, here the men are, and it is ludicrous to attribute their joblessness to corporate bigotry rather than to their own unemployability. The high school dropout rate in Cincinnati is between 60 and 70 percent. And will the young men across from Johnnie's show up every day to work on time and respond appropriately to authority? Has any of them even applied for a job and been turned down? Last summer King's Island, an amusement park north of the city, had to import 1,000 young Eastern Europeans for summer jobs because it could find no local youths to apply. Yet the well-intentioned CEO of Procter & Gamble, Cincinnati's beloved corporate titan, has called, in good riot-ideologue fashion, for the urgent creation of 2,500 government- and privately subsidized summer jobs to forestall another rampage.

I asked Ross Love what evidence he had for "economic exclusion" in Cincinnati. "You have to look at the end result," he said. "The unemployment rate is four times higher for blacks than for whites; for 18- to 30-year-olds, it is an incredible 50 percent." But "looking at the end result" is the hallmark of bogus civil rights analysis, designed to shift attention from individual deficits onto the resultant disparate outcomes, which are then attributed to racism. We can argue about whether society is, in some structural way, still somehow to blame for Cincinnati's idle, functionally illiterate young dealers, but let's not brand employers as racist.

Cincinnati's African immigrants have a different perspective from CAN on "economic exclusion." "We experience more resentment from African-Americans than from whites," says cabdriver Mor Thiam. "They don't want to see us in business. 'Man, go back to Africa! You come here and take our monies,' they say." Amy, a

Senegalese cabdriver in a robin's-egg-blue ruffled cotton dress, has been teaching herself about riot ideology by listening to Ross Love's local radio station, WDBZ, "The Buzz." "They are angry on that station!" she exclaims. "A lot of them don't work; they go to your taxi, try to steal your money. When I came here, I earned $4.25 an hour, but I worked. I liked it. I paid my bills; I sent money home. If you want to get a job, you get a job. We see a lot of opportunity here."

The notion that this friendly, well-meaning town is denying employment to job-ready black men because of the color of their skin is ridiculous. To the contrary, Cincinnati's biggest corporations have long practiced affirmative action. Expect CAN's "economic inclusion" task force to recommend even more quotas, however, rather than honestly to address why young blacks are not working.

Those who attribute riots to racism blame racist police no less than racist employers. The riot apologists' most incessant indictment against the Cincinnati Police Division: the Cincinnati fifteen. But besides ignoring the defensive nature of almost all the killings, the apologists never mention that one of the fifteen victims dragged an officer—a black officer—to his death in a car; or that, as of May 17, all four of the most recent shootings by police (two lethal) involved black officers; or that, with a death toll of three officers over the last four years, a Cincinnati cop is twenty-seven times more likely to die at the hands of a black man than a black man is to die at the hands of the Cincinnati police.

Little evidence supports the claim that the Cincinnati Police Division is an institution out of control. In 1999 Cincinnati officers had fewer fatal shootings per officer than the San Diego Police Department, constantly lauded as progressive by the liberal press. Over the last six years the police in St. Louis, a city comparable in size to Cincinnati, killed twenty suspects, according to the *Cincinnati Enquirer*, without attracting the national media's attention.

Cincinnati officers use nonlethal physical force (such as punching or kicking) about fifty times per year, or in .09 percent of all arrests: an unexceptionable rate. A *Cincinnati Enquirer* study found no racial pattern in force incidents, and as for the racial profiling charges, Cincinnati officers ticket black and white drivers proportionately to their representation in the city's population. The department's current and previous chief are highly respected among their peers. While by no means as cutting-edge in its management techniques as the New York Police Department, the Cincinnati department appears to be easily as well managed as most.

Like every police force in the country, the Cincinnati department struggles with police-community relations. Too many officers are sullen and defensive, say some downtown leaders. Of course, they often face a very hostile audience. "Younger people have a hateful attitude," laments Officer Dean Chatman, recalling the f—k-the-police T-shirts he has seen. Boys try to provoke the police into chasing them, so that they can be caught empty-handed. Passersby often accuse Chatman of being a "house nigger." "They tell me: 'You've sold out; you especially should understand,'" he says. "My response is: 'No, I don't. My brother wouldn't do what you're doing.'"

But for all the talk of Cincinnati's abysmal police-community relations, it is easy to find people who bear no animus toward the police. Typical is Galen Bailey, a forty-year-old illustrator. He figures he's been stopped fifteen or sixteen times for speeding (he drives very fast), and there has been a warrant out for his arrest because of unpaid traffic tickets. The only time he's felt any qualms about a police officer occurred during a traffic stop across the Ohio River in Kentucky: "I got the impression I should keep my mouth shut," he recalls.

Even some of those who express animus report civil treatment. A sixteen-year-old in a do-rag and low-slung pants waiting at a bus stop outside City Hall says he figures he's had three encounters with the police. Most recently he was frisked by officers looking for car thieves. Afterward they said: "We're sorry, we made a terrible mistake"—precisely the courtesy that police brass nationally struggle to elicit from their officers. The apology calmed him down a little, he said, "but they still had me kind of mad."

But the Cincinnati Police Division does have one very big problem: it has to fight too hard to get rid of bad apples on the force. About a decade ago, seeking to give managers more power, the department instituted binding arbitration for disciplining officers. "It was the worst thing we've ever done," says former police chief Mike Snowdon. The arbitrators almost always vote pro-union and anti-management; the division has lost all of its last ten cases. Rolando Underwood is the poster boy for the department's discipline problems. A 6-foot-2, 245-pound drug dealer, Underwood was suspended three times, fired and reinstated once, and reprimanded five times for offenses ranging from incompetence to neglect of duty during his ten years on the force. In 1995 he was suspended for conduct unbecoming to an officer for a sexual imbroglio. The department finally nailed him when he negotiated an $80,000 marijuana deal with an undercover officer.

No protesters are calling for giving management more power to fight police corruption, however; instead, the activists are making the usual demands for stronger civilian oversight. And they are racializing the discipline issue. In 1995 a special commission decried the fact that blacks, 23 percent of the force, represented 44 percent of all discipline cases. But court mandates have forced Cincinnati to hire and promote by race since 1981, and of course such mandates invariably compromise quality.

Even so, the department is far from the pit of injustice that the civil rights establishment and the national press have painted it. Does it stop and frisk more blacks than whites? You bet: because blacks commit the overwhelming preponderance of crime in Cincinnati. Bringing up that issue, however, is deemed "racially inflammatory." But it wasn't police brutality that incited the riots; it was the incessant anti-police campaign waged by local activists.

Ever since the Kerner Commission report, riot apologists have insisted that more social programs are necessary to prevent riots. The Kerner Commission called for welfare on demand, one million new government jobs, and extensive new job-training programs. No matter that the federal government was already spending $1.6 billion on job training in 1968, that cities with some of the most brutal riots, such as Detroit and New Haven, were particularly well-endowed with more than four hundred federal poverty programs, or that the welfare population was already skyrocketing, despite an unprecedentedly long period of economic growth.

Cincinnati's leaders are no less impervious to reality. Since the riots, the Reverend Damon Lynch has been blaming "disinvestment" in poorer areas and demanding that poverty agencies that had been defunded because of fraud be fully refunded. Yet Over-the-Rhine, with its thick concentration of helping agencies, is already a social worker's dream.

Mayor Luken's swipe at the business community, with its faux sorrow and its faux facts, is a riot-ideology classic. "I am somewhat saddened that it takes this kind of situation to come together, [but] I'm happy that business leaders are finally engaged," he pontificated at the end of riot week. Finally engaged? Cincinnati's business community can perhaps be faulted for the dreary conventionality and naiveté of its philanthropic efforts but not for the scope of those efforts. Local corporations contribute millions to poverty agencies and civil rights groups. Fifth Third Bancorp and Procter & Gamble, for example, have been funding "economic development" in Walnut Hills, home of Johnnie's Supermarket, only to see their projects torn up by the recent riots. Loath to bear a grudge, the companies have only "redoubled [their] commitment to . . . improve the neighborhood," according to a spokesman. Too bad they haven't decided to rethink radically what Walnut Hills and other riot targets really need.

Rioting sends a message, according to the riot ideology. Indeed, riot apologists attribute deep thoughts about injustice to vandals. An assistant professor of communication at the University of

Cincinnati saw the recent riots as a campfire sing-along: "People wanted to come together and express their solidarity and frustration and outrage," he explained. David Gergen of *U.S. News & World Report* discerned concerns about global capitalism in the bonfires of Over-the-Rhine. The *Cincinnati Enquirer* was an equally creative oracle: the riots "revealed dissatisfaction in the areas of education, jobs, and economic opportunity," it editorialized.

These sympathetic spokesmen overlook one hard fact: rioters are often criminals. Seventy-two percent of the defendants indicted so far in the Cincinnati explosion have adult criminal histories. Prior offenses include rape, aggravated robbery, aggravated burglary, assault, weapons discharge, and endangering children. The Walnut Hills riot was started by drug dealers and their clients, according to Candace Tubbs, a convicted former assistant to a Cincinnati drug lord who described to me the fun she used to have rolling in the piles of cash her boss hauled in. These rioting felons were simply wreaking en masse the destruction they usually wreak individually.

Many riot skeptics, including the great Edward Banfield, have questioned the logic of protesting injustice by destroying your local grocery store, or fighting police brutality by stealing microwave ovens. The riot apologists who nominate inadequate social spending as a "root cause" should wonder what "message" the Cincinnati rioters were sending when they torched poverty agencies. One group that provided financial assistance and job training, for example, lost about $50,000 from fire and theft.

No one likes alarm clocks, but we all acknowledge their usefulness. So too with riots, according to the true believers. CAN's Ross Love told me that the "unrest" was a "wake-up call that the city needed." Kenneth Lawson, the inflammatory anti-police attorney, explained that the beatings of whites provided their recipients a lesson in what the "brothers" experience daily from the police, and that presumably the white establishment would take notice.

The *Los Angeles Times* oozed: "While no one wants to say that the riots were good, there was on Friday an undeniable sense of relief that the mayhem . . . had laid bare Cincinnati's fissures. Now, perhaps, there could be progress."

Try telling Chris Schoonover how useful rioting is. Schoonover is part of a still-small movement of white residents and business owners back into Over-the-Rhine. On the first day of violence, as she was driving back to her apartment, a brick flew through the car's open window and struck her. "Man, you hit her in the head!" one brick thrower admiringly exclaimed to his buddy. At the hospital, Schoonover recognized an acquaintance among the dozens of bloodied people waiting for care: a rioter had jumped into her acquaintance's car and beaten her viciously with a brick.

Since the attack, which left five staples in her scalp, Schoonover's world has changed completely. Once exquisitely sensitive to racial political correctness, she now sees the world in black and white. For days after the attack she was terrified to return to her largely black neighborhood and university. The sight of white girls jogging alone filled her with dread that they would be attacked by a black person.

This heightened racial mistrust runs both ways. Schoonover's black colleagues at the bar where she works were clearly uncomfortable around her after the riots. "The black community had put out a call to arms: 'We need to be strong and united,'" she says. The call translated into greater separatism.

After a couple of postriot incidents in which white friends were threatened, Schoonover has blacked out her window so people on the street won't see a white girl alone in her apartment. She recalls that, after the brick attack, "I was crying, because this was my neighborhood"—"her" neighborhood, despite the crack whores and the young men hustling drugs. Now she's not so sure.

Here is the hidden logic of race riots: supposedly a cry against racial oppression, their implicit threat to destroy the city merely guarantees full employment for race hustlers and sensitivity trainers by driving the races further apart. If whites flee Over-the-Rhine, expect plenty of breast-beating in the future from the press and civil rights advocates about Cincinnati's enduring racial segregation. No one will recall why the integrators left.

Riot apologists even deny the economic damage they cause. "No one has lost property value because of the riots," Ross Love told me. "Property values have gone up since the 1960s riots; there's no reason to believe values are down because of last April."

"Is he crazy? What is he talking about?" sputtered Marlene Vonderhaar, an Over-the-Rhine merchant, when I told her of Love's claims. In all of May, Vonderhaar made two sales from her antique store. "My shop is dead," she pronounces. Suburban customers refuse to come downtown now; business in the area has dropped some 60 percent. Vonderhaar lost up to $50,000 in merchandise when vandals, enraged that her store was already boarded up, hurled tires and bricks against the plywood, sending mirrors and ceramics shattering to the floor.

Vonderhaar's antique store typifies the "gentrification" that some media critics blame for the riots. So what will be lost if her store and others like it fold? The new Over-the-Rhine entrepreneurs offer jobs to those local residents who have the work ethic to take advantage of them. They provide entree to the world of work beyond Over-the-Rhine. And sometimes they may try on a very personal level to free someone from the ghetto. For several years Vonderhaar has been struggling to save from the streets a charming homosexual youth with a crack-addicted mother. After he stole money from her, Vonderhaar gave him a second chance and tried hard to help. But when he continued to steal from her and others, she finally gave up. "He broke my heart and broke me," she says.

According to the riot ideology, the most authentic black leaders are angry black leaders, and the Reverend Damon Lynch, ever since his appointment as the city's Number One racial healer, has taken on the role with a vengeance. He drove out an annual rock festival from Over-the-Rhine by threatening boycotts and protests, and he tried to shut down one of Cincinnati's most moneymaking tourist attractions, its food festival. During a noisy sit-in at a downtown restaurant, he promised to "let people know that Cincinnati is not a place to bring your conventions or your business. Until there is justice, there will be no business as usual, no lunch as usual." (Lynch carefully refrained from defining the "justice" that would buy peace.) His choice of protest symbolism was fanciful, since no one has ever alleged that blacks cannot get service at downtown restaurants—but no more fanciful than his comparison of Cincinnati to South Africa in its "economic apartheid."

Lynch's rhetorical extremism guarantees his ongoing relevance as anointed black leader. Liberal whites need black anger to prove the persistence of racism among their unenlightened neighbors, which they alone can atone for by the noblesse oblige of liberal paternalism. Thus, to reinforce their own sense of moral superiority, they confer racial authenticity only on blacks like Damon Lynch, self-proclaimed angry victims of American bigotry. Lynch's ever more rash protests make a mockery of his mediator position on Community Action Now; if he wants to continue playing firebrand, he should resign from CAN. But no one dares suggest he leave, even though his boycotts are killing the very neighborhood he purports to represent. Ross Love's support of his co-chair reflects his grasp of the underlying dialectic: "Lynch's protests increase his authority," he told me. "They give him more credibility in the eyes of the people we need at the table."

And here, in a nutshell, is the tragedy of moral leadership in black America. Love merely states received wisdom in claiming that black moral authority derives from protesting white racism, and that the alienated youth who most respond to such protests are the most authentic representatives of the black community.

This logic consigns to silence many, many black Americans—law-abiding citizens who see crime, not racism, as the biggest threat in their lives. Over-the-Rhine resident Sheila Randle, for example, doesn't buy Love's and Lynch's charges. A former manager of Salvation Army stores, the fifty-year-old Randle is a prisoner in her own home. Young people smoke marijuana and crack on the street outside her apartment all night; they jeer at her husband when he asks them to get off his car. Addicts have started breaking into her building's entryway. "You never know who's going to be on the landing in the morning," she says. Randle is desperate to move, but her options are limited.

What about these stories of police racism? I ask her. "I have no problem with the police; they treat me respectfully," she answers. "It's the young people who are the problem." And the thesis that the police only care about white yuppies? "The police are there to protect all the people, not just the whites," she asserts. What about societal racism generally? "I've never experienced it."

Randle wanted to support the police in their time of trouble by attending the annual police memorial this May. The anti-police demonstrators frightened her off, however—demonstrators allegedly representing her interests as an oppressed black woman. As for the claim that the Timothy Thomas shooting is a sign of police racism, Randle will have none of it. "Thomas brought it on himself," she says. "He had [warrants] on him; if he had halted like they told him to, it wouldn't have happened."

This is no fringe view. In early May a letter writer named Loretta Blackburn wrote to the *Cincinnati Enquirer*: "If I were in pursuit of a black youth and had cornered him in an alley, after what happened to Officer Kevin Crayon [dragged to death last year by a twelve-year-old joyrider], the first thing in my mind would be, 'Someone is coming out of this alley; now who do you think it will be?' We as black people need to get back to the basics and help the police to police our neighborhoods. . . . When you are in the streets hollering how unfair black people are being treated, what are you teaching your children about respect for authority? If you don't like the job that [the police] are doing, then give them a helping hand, not a shot in the back."

Damon Lynch, Al Sharpton, and Kweisi Mfume have no interest in representing the Sheila Randles and Loretta Blackburns. Far more responsible leaders who do speak for such citizens are out there, though—but the opinion elites are not about to give them a platform.

Tom Jones is standing arms akimbo just inside Johnnie's Supermarket, the beleaguered shooting target in Walnut Hills. Jones is helping Johnnie's landlord, William "Babe" Baker, put the store back on its feet after police busted its previous Arab lessees for fencing stolen goods. A small, wiry man in his fifties, alternately serious and effervescent, Jones is arguably the most relentless advocate for public safety in Cincinnati. Since moving his copying business here in 1995 from Washington, D.C., he has been organizing his community to battle drug dealers. His efforts helped cops make 335 drug arrests in a three-month period in 1999.

Jones has one overriding principle for how to take back a community from crime: "You must build a working relationship with the police," he says, crouching down for emphasis. Jones taught his fellow businessmen in Avondale, the still-scarred epicenter of the 1968 riots, to call the police when crowds of dealers amassed in front of their stores. "They weren't calling!" he recalls in amazement. He organized a crime task force that won extra police patrols for the district. Unable to persuade the merchants to testify in drug cases, Jones goes on their behalf. "I stand in front of the judge and tell him: 'This community wants the dealers out,'" he says.

Jones's work with the police has won him accolades and, by a landslide, the presidency of the local community council, but he has acquired numerous enemies as well. "I may as well have KKK written on my chest," he says. Sure enough, when I asked members of the Special Forces, the black nationalists who have been disrupting the City Council, about Tom Jones, one of their "generals" contemptuously replied: "Oh, you mean Uncle Tom Jones? He was with his little group to sterilize Burnet Avenue [Avondale's main commercial strip]. We don't need police protection; it was only one block, and most of the crime is gone." Not exactly. Last year a drug dealer fatally shot a landlord in the head on Burnet Avenue for removing the dealers from his property. Jones has been shot at as well.

Jones has only scorn for the postriot circus. Would the civil rights activists and poverty advocates on CAN's six task forces show up if they couldn't get a cut of the resulting money? he wonders. As for that beefed-up social spending, Jones observes that "developed neighborhoods work very well without social programs, because they got up off their ass and solved their problems." If the existing programs didn't prevent the riots, Jones asks, "Why are we creating more programs?"

No less iconoclastic is the man Jones is helping at Johnnie's— real-estate owner Babe Baker. Infuriating the black establishment is a badge of honor for these men. "I'm probably the most disliked person in this city," Baker says proudly. "No, you're not; I am!" Tom Jones shoots back, laughing.

Actually, it's hard to imagine anyone disliking the tall, ebullient eighty-four-year-old Baker, a former luminary of Cincinnati's rich musical life. In the 1950s and 1960s Baker was the impresario for serious jazz in Cincinnati, booking such greats as John Coltrane and Cannonball Adderley into his dozen nightclubs. But the 1968 riots almost bankrupted him, and now he sees the same destructive rationalizations for violence at work again. "You can't go around with a chip on your shoulder, blaming the world for your problems," he says of the rioters. "You must have a desire to do something." Black poverty will be solved only by "education and economics—putting your shoulder to the workforce"—not by protests, he insists.

Baker embodies a powerful tradition in black culture: optimistic self-help. Arriving in Cincinnati from Alabama at age eleven, he started working in a produce market in Over-the-Rhine and has not stopped working since. I ask him if there was a different work ethic back then. He closes his eyes and laughs uproariously. Pausing to wipe his eyes, he answers in a voice high and scratchy with age: "Absolutely! I've done all sorts of work. When I drove cabs, the other drivers taught me to trip the meter. I refused to do it, and they wonder why I made it and they didn't." Welfare destroyed self-reliance, he says, and resulted in the time bomb of "babies having babies."

Baker believes that the free market is the best chance for reviving Over-the-Rhine and other troubled areas. He is a font of the entrepreneurial wisdom needed to do it. "You must pay your bills!" he says. After the 1968 riots he obtained a loan to keep his jazz clubs open, but eventually the bank wrote it off. Five years later he reactivated his debt and repaid it in full. Later, he wanted to buy some property for $80,000. "I went back to the bank and asked how to finance it. 'Mr. Baker, with your signature,' they said. Today I can borrow more money than I need."

He knows how crucial knowledge is and frets that aspiring black entrepreneurs are reluctant to seek it. "You know how I learned banking?" he asks. "Someone asked me for a financial statement. I didn't know what one was. I asked: 'Will you please explain to me what that means?' All you have to do is be honest, not smart-alecky, and say to people: 'I really don't understand,' and they will help you," he says enthusiastically. And like any entrepreneur, he takes for granted the need to save and invest. "The mistakes we made?" Baker muses. "When we made a little money, we bought a Cadillac, not a house."

Don't wait for Baker to get a hearing in official Cincinnati; his views are just too radical. Most galling, he denies the charge of systemic racism. "This used to be a prejudiced city, but that's changed," he says. "Blacks are making lots of money now." The racial profiling controversy? He's not buying it. "I'm a disciplinarian. There's no reason to get into trouble."

What a difference it would make if Jones were as lionized for suppressing the drug trade on Burnet Avenue as Damon Lynch is for organizing boycotts, or if the press gave legitimacy to people like Jones and Babe Baker instead of to Jesse Jackson and Al Sharpton. If the media did pay attention to the racial nonconformists, it would find a large, untapped audience, frustrated with conventional black politics but also afraid of retribution for dissent. A downtown Cincinnati business figure who would only speak anonymously told me bitterly: "The civil rights leadership is killing us; it's absolutely killing us. As white exploitation is a sin, so is black waste. We are living in an unnatural state." Illustrator Galen Bailey blames Lynch and Lawson's preriot rabble-rousing for the violence: "All these young kids needed was for an adult to give them permission to riot," he says in dismay.

Riot ideology in Cincinnati has had its usual effect. In the month following the riots, violent crime of all kinds rocketed up 20 percent. This is not surprising. Not only did the riot ideologists romanticize assaults and theft as a long-overdue blow for justice, but they demonized the police as hard-core racists. Arrests for quality-of-life offenses, disorderly conduct, and drug possession—the firewall against more serious crime—have plummeted since the riots, as the police keep their heads down.

The next time an urban riot hits, the best response is: do nothing. Compensate the property owners, then shut up. Scurrying around with anti-racism task forces and aid packages tells young kids: this is the way to get the world to notice you, this is power—destruction, instead of staying in school, studying, and accomplishing something lawful. Even better, of course, would be to prevent the next riot before it happens by sending in police in force at the first sign of trouble.

But better even than this, political and business leaders who have not already sold out to the civil rights monopolists should try to break their cartel. They should find black citizens who are willing to speak about values and personal responsibility, and who embody them in their own lives. They should appear with these citizens at public meetings and put them on task forces, if task forces they must have. If they do it enough, the press will have to pay attention. And when the voice of hardworking black America becomes familiar, the riot ideology may finally lose its death grip on American politics.

Wrong on the Facts

THE NEW REPUBLIC'S Michelle Cottle has given riot ideology a decidedly new-century twist: economic revitalization, not economic abandonment, in Over-the-Rhine caused the Cincinnati riots, she argues. Seems you just can't win.

Cottle's anti-gentrification case is easily dismissable, since growth is an antidote to, not a cause of, poverty. But buried in her occasionally qualified case against development is something far more dangerous: a spurious revisionist history of 1990s policing that seeks to delegitimate the greatest crime conquest—and the greatest boon to the law-abiding majority of ghetto residents—in decades.

Cottle stops just short of claiming that the new businesses and few white residents trickling into Over-the-Rhine have actually displaced black residents. She is wise to restrain herself. In 1870 Over-the-Rhine housed 60,000; today, the same buildings contain just over 7,600 people, 20 percent fewer than in 1990. There's room and to spare.

The biggest problem with new urban entrepreneurship, Cottle asserts, is that it brings in the police. Cottle claims that 1990s policing in Cincinnati, New York, and elsewhere arose from the need to make the world safe for white yuppies. If the police stopped and frisked more suspects for guns, if they enforced quality-of-life ordinances more vigorously—enforcement techniques she preposterously labels "police brutality"—it was only to protect the white urban homesteaders moving into the ghetto.

This is fantasy of the purest order. Had Cottle bothered to check the facts, she would have discovered that policing in the

1990s was driven by one thing and one thing only: the incidence of crime. There is no column in the reams of data that top brass pore over in New York's weekly Compstat meetings for neighborhood Starbucks, no column for the social class of crime victims. A Compstat session several months ago intensely grilled a Queens borough commander over the murder of a Mexican gangbanger outside a seedy bar; no one asked first whether white dot-commers had "discovered" the bar. The most stunning crime drops in New York occurred in places like the 33rd and 34th Precincts in Washington Heights—heart of the Dominican drug industry and a neighborhood wholly unspoiled by Martha Stewart catalogs. The NYPD created Model Blocks—its most intensive policing strategy, designed to liberate law-abiding residents from drug dealers—only in ungentrified neighborhoods. Cottle could stand a very long time on Elder Avenue, a Model Block in the Bronx, without seeing a single white person—with or without a Ralph Lauren polo shirt.

The situation in Cincinnati and other cities that implemented data-driven policing is the same. Police go where the crime is, and that is almost invariably in minority communities. But unfortunately Cottle's ignorant thesis is catching on; of course the *New York Times* promptly picked it up, as part of the liberal press's ongoing effort to discredit as racist the policing revolution of the last decade. If that effort succeeds, the long abatement of crime will end, and inner-city neighborhoods will return to the reign of the thugs.

2001

The Black Cops You Never Hear About

ASK DETECTIVE CARL MCLAUGHLIN if the police prey on black people, and this normally ebullient Brooklyn cop will respond icily: "I just prey on people that are preying on others. It shouldn't be a race thing."

A cop's denial that policing is racist is perhaps not noteworthy—except for one thing: Detective McLaughlin is himself black. As such, he represents an ignored constituency in contemporary policing controversies: black officers who loathe race-based cop-bashing as much as any Irish flatfoot. As the ACLU and other professional cop-haters flood the media with tales of endemic police racism, rank-and-file minority officers, who might be considered ideal commentators on these matters, appear only as intriguing statistics—such as those showing that black state troopers in New Jersey, the alleged cradle of racial profiling, stop the same proportion of black drivers as do their purportedly racist white colleagues.

So I set out to talk to black cops and commanders from eight police departments across the country about why they became policemen and how they view today's policing controversies. What I found was a bracing commitment to law and order, a resounding rejection of anti-cop propaganda, and a conviction that racial politics are a tragic drag on black progress. The thoroughly mainstream views of these black cops are a reminder that invisible behind the antics of Al Sharpton and Jesse Jackson are many black citizens who share the commonsense values of most Americans.

Tony Barksdale's epiphany about policing came while he was a poli-sci student at Baltimore's Coppin State College in 1993. "I saw these officers bail out of their car and start chasing a guy," he recalls. "They were black guys chasing the perp, and they were young. Right then and there, I just felt it. I said, 'Wow! That's where you should be. That's the uniform you should wear.'" Barksdale dropped out of college to join the Baltimore force, to the horror of his mother—and his girlfriend, who dumped him on the spot. He has had his vindication: his ex-girlfriend's mother saw him hobnobbing with the police commissioner recently. "She was ready to kill herself," he gloats.

Barksdale has shot up through the ranks of the Baltimore Police Department under the meritocratic regime of Commissioner Ed Norris, a recruit from the hard-charging Compstat-era NYPD. While Detective Barksdale was still a sergeant, Norris noticed his success in clearing big drug cases and offered him a citywide drug unit. "No thanks," Barksdale told him. "I have a squad of guys who are loyal to me." "Loyalty," Norris responded. "I like that." Then, blithely ignoring Barksdale's demurral, he ordered: "Report on Monday." Now a lieutenant, Barksdale, along with his sixteen detectives and two sergeants, has been pulling drugs and guns off Baltimore's crime-ridden streets at an impressive rate. "I've never regretted my decision," he says. "I still get excited every day."

The enthusiasm that brought Barksdale into policing is typical of younger black officers. "I wanted to always become a police officer," explains David Brown, a rookie cop in downtown Brooklyn. "I had always had the mentality of the good and the just." Lieutenant Mark Christian, a self-described "military brat" who now heads the SWAT, hostage negotiation, and canine units in San Antonio, Texas, picked up the love of "service and the uniform" from his air force–veteran father.

The reason some older black policemen pinned on the badge could not be more different. "I became a cop because I couldn't stand 'em," recalls William Hubbard, who joined the NYPD in the 1960s, after being treated harshly by officers around the Queens projects where he grew up. Yet even in Hubbard's generation, such motivating anger was by no means universal. Blacks have served proudly as cops since the early nineteenth century, despite often humiliating second-class status within their departments. Philadelphia sergeant Aisha Perry's grandfather was a Philly officer when the department was still segregated, yet he loved his job. "We always felt policing was admirable work," she says. Police work also offered blacks security and a hope for middle-class status long before the corporate world opened up to them.

But all black officers, whatever their reason for joining the force, face the same occupational hazard: race-based taunting. "You work for the man!" Detective Carl McLaughlin constantly hears in Brooklyn. "I don't work for 'the man,'" he says impatiently. "I work for the penal law." The taunts have become "more sophisticated" over the years, McLaughlin reports. "They use bigger words. 'Because of you, I'm going to get reparations!' they shout." McLaughlin smiles beatifically back, the soul of innocence: "Me too: I'm black!" Detective Robert Reedy, a heavy-smoking mountain of a man in an aquamarine pin striped suit, works with McLaughlin in the 67th Precinct. "They call me a slave, a field nigger," he says. He responds contemptuously: "That's 'house nigger'—get your terms right." The perps then whine: "You black like me!" Reedy shakes his head in amazement: "What's that got to do with taking the lady's handbag?"

Then the wheedling begins. "It's hard on the streets," the thugs complain. "Get a job at McDonald's," Reedy replies. Reedy himself ran with delinquents growing up in the East New York projects. When he started training in the police academy, his friends would mockingly smoke marijuana in front of him and sneer: "What you gonna do to me?" Now, however, they respect his success, even as they stay stuck in the underclass.

Some officers try to talk sense into the taunters. Every time Troy Smith, a hostage negotiator in San Antonio, hears: "Aw, c'mon, bro', you tryin' to keep us down," he replies: "You have to make your own way. You make excuses, you'll never get anywhere." Other officers, however, refuse to take the bait. When San Antonio's Lieutenant Christian is accused of selling out and working for the man, "I don't smile at them or rise to it," he says. "They think they can drive a wedge between us and the department." Such insults have accompanied black police work for all of living memory. A 1969 study of black policemen, for example, recounted the abuse they received from "lower-class Negro youth." One New York officer confessed: "When they talk like this: 'How about giving me a break, I'm colored, too,' . . . they get a ticket right away. No doubt about it. A real quick summons."

Though officers report these sallies with scorn, they still wince at them. "Sometimes it hurts your feelings," admits Detective McLaughlin. The riffraff know where the soft spots are and aim at them with insults about, for example, the Abner Louima incident. "Your friends stick it up the ass!" they jeer. "The cop who assaulted Louima was wrong," McLaughlin says in frustration. "He made all of us look bad. What about all the people you don't shoot?" This usually upbeat Brooklyn detective sighs: "It's really hard now. Anyone can say: 'You fuckin' cops, you fuckin' cops, I pay your salary.' You have to be a doctor, a psychiatrist, a bad guy, and a good guy in one minute. You have to understand the plight of the black man, the plight of women, the plight of gays, and not piss someone off and lose your job, all in the course of a day."

The post-9/11 spurt of patriotism provided a brief respite from these pressures. "The best time to be a cop was with Elliot Ness [the federal agent who stopped Al Capone] and after September

11," muses McLaughlin. After 9/11 "people would say: 'I love you'; they were naming their kids after you," he recalls with a big smile. "It went from 'Motherfucker' to 'Mister.'" Were you bitter? I ask him. He shakes his head. "I was just shocked. These people were bizarre, clapping every time they saw you. I went on a cruise and a woman asked to give me a hug." Such gratitude was short-lived, however. Three months later—in Flatbush, at least—it's back to "Motherfucker."

Occasionally the racial taunting pays off. When some officers hear, "You're one of us; you're selling out," they take it to heart, according to San Antonio's Lieutenant Christian. "You'll see their mindset change; they make sideways comments about the police department. 'It's the department versus the citizens,' they'll say— treating the department as a monolith. The pressures brought to bear by 'the community' on black officers can make them less effective," Christian observes. But most simply redouble their crime-fighting efforts against "the knuckleheads" on behalf of the "good people."

It is their emotional relation to the "good people" of the community that makes policing such an imperative for these cops. Many come from God-fearing, law-abiding homes where respect for authority was absolute. Reedy's mother warned him when he was young that if she ever got a call about him from the police, he shouldn't call her, he should call the funeral home. These officers have seen firsthand the damage done by thugs, and they are determined to stop it. "I will never retreat," vows McLaughlin. "We are the last line of defense against mayhem." Amid all the anti-cop taunting they hear, they remind themselves, in the words of Officer David Brown, that crime victims "regard you as heroes."

If the law-abiding black poor and middle class are no abstractions for these cops—as they are for guilty white liberals, who condescendingly think they are benefiting "black people" by promoting criminal-friendly policies—neither is the depravity of young thugs some distant construct to be brushed away for the more gratifying exercise of "understanding the underprivileged." "Their values are so screwed up," says Steve Hector, a quiet, pot-bellied Brooklyn detective, whose dreadlocks are swept up in a top-knot. "This is a lost generation: the value of life doesn't mean shit for them."

Hector's colleague Reedy nods and offers an example that he says brought him almost to tears. A seventeen-year-old dealer was smoking blunts with a friend, whom he then accused of owing him money. To emphasize his demand, he shot the debtor. The dealer then put his gun to his fallen victim's head and blew his brains out, securing in an instant his reputation for toughness on the street. In the squad car, Reedy recalls, the murderer acted as if the whole affair was a joke. "He was singing Jay-Z songs," Reedy marvels. During questioning in the station house, Reedy challenged him: "I don't believe you murdered someone." The teen looked him in the eye and spat back: "I'd murder you!" "I was shaking," Reedy remembers. "I said to myself: 'He's psycho!'"

Constant exposure to criminals teaches cops how to recognize them. "Just as we stand out, they stand out," explains San Antonio's Troy Smith. But being black by no means insulates officers from the racial profiling charge when they arrest a lowlife they've spotted. "You're locking me up because I'm black," criminals tell Detective McLaughlin. "I'm locking you up because you're wrong," he responds.

Nor is it just hardened thugs who charge black cops with racial profiling. In Washington State, former trooper and state legislator John Lovick publicly accused Deputy Dallas Hogan of making a race-based stop. Shot back Hogan: "Lovick is a disgrace to the profession, and right now he is a disgrace to my race." The legislator had been driving fifteen miles an hour under the speed limit after midnight. Hogan ran the plates and discovered that the car's owner had relinquished his license because of old age. Fearful that the driver, whom he couldn't see, might be the old man, lost or with Alzheimer's, Hogan pulled the car over for a safety check. The legislator immediately cried racism. "Lovick has a chip on his shoulder the size of Texas," says Hogan testily. "He believes any contact with law enforcement is based on race."

Most officers I spoke to reject the racial profiling myth. If you're stopped, said these policemen, it's for a reason—you fit a description, or you've done something to raise an officer's suspicion, such as hitch up your waistband in a way that suggests a hidden gun. Statistics that tabulate officer-civilian interactions by race alone grossly distort the reality of policing, complain many black cops. "You have to look at time, place, and situation," observes San Antonio's Lieutenant Christian. "You know what goes on at that corner. If someone's hanging out with a known offender, ethnicity is the last thing that comes into play."

These cops scoff at the ACLU's charge that a black driver who has not been harassed because of his skin color is an "aberration." Bridgeport chief Wilbur Chapman says he has been stopped "a few times, to say the least." Why? "I speed," he laughs. "I inherited it from my father." During one stop, while Chapman was out of uniform, his son blurted out to the trooper that his daddy too had a gun. "The cop politely said: 'Excuse me, sir, do you have registration for your gun?' I wasn't thrown against the hood; I couldn't have been treated nicer. Those of us without an ax to grind have stories like these aplenty," Chapman asserts.

The racial profiling myth rests on a willful blindness to reality, say many black cops. "We're so afraid to tell the truth," complains Lieutenant Barksdale. "Often the entire neighborhood is black, so of course you're going to be stopping blacks—based on their behavior." The racial backlash sparked by many anti-crime initiatives "conveniently ignores" one salient fact, says Lieutenant Christian: "Most crime against blacks is committed by blacks, not Anglos or Hispanics."

The costs of the racial profiling crusade, warn these officers, are enormous. Barksdale notes that an officer who hears, "You only stopped me because I'm black," may well be inhibited from taking further necessary action or from making future stops. "But how do you know that the complainer hasn't just shot someone, or has a secret compartment [for drugs or guns]?" he wonders. Unless top management reassures cops that they can count on support in strong enforcement actions, black officers caution, some policemen will inevitably back off in the face of racial pressures. Witness what happened in Cincinnati and New Jersey after relentless race-based anti-cop campaigns. In 2001 Cincinnati experienced the bloodiest summer in its history, as stops and arrests plummeted. In New Jersey, consent searches for guns and drugs on the turnpike plunged in the six months that ended October 31, 2001. Drug traffickers sailed through the turnpike unimpeded while murder in Newark jumped 65 percent in 2001.

But the racial profiling juggernaut is just one part of a broader attack on policing that makes the job increasingly difficult, lament many black officers. They complain about the second-guessing of police actions and the zero tolerance for error. "One of the problems we have today," observes New York's David Brown, "is so much media. Everyone has a camcorder, and they edit it to their advantage. Bystanders will say: 'Why is this police officer doing this to this person?'—even if they arrived at the scene five or ten seconds later, and this is a really, really bad guy. You're trying to apprehend a bad guy and you break his arm. Now you're the bad guy? But if he gets your gun, he'll try to shoot someone: so is that excessive force? Say someone gets shot. Who do they go after—the perp or the cop? It won't be the perp, because no one wants to deal with the bad guy. If you think about this every day, you go crazy, so you can't. You won't be policing; you'll be out there scared to death, paranoid about everything."

From the firearms-discharge review process to civilian-complaint review boards, black cops, like their peers of all races, feel that they, not the criminals, bear all the weight of public suspicion. "After you discharge your weapon, you think: 'Now this job is coming to get me,'" says Detective Robert Reedy. "This job makes you feel guilty until proven innocent." All the cops I spoke to reject the notion that the shooting of Amadou Diallo had anything to do with race. The public should try to understand the life-and-death pressures they face, they suggest. "With a situation like Diallo, you have to make a split-second decision, and it can change your life," says McLaughlin. Sometimes officers make mistakes, acknowledges David Brown. "But do you hold them liable as racist persons? That's where the stress comes from: you can't make mistakes."

Cops—black, white, Hispanic, you name it—scratch their heads at the seeming priorities of "the community." "There can be 50 shootings of civilians, and no one will protest," marvels John Hayward, a fast-talking community-response officer from the Philadelphia department. "If a cop shoots one person, everyone's demonstrating. If you protest against us, why don't you protest against the drug dealers?" Cops also notice the strangely variable perceptions of civilians. "Some blacks who complain about the police—they'll see it if an officer shoots someone three blocks away," chuckles Detective Reedy. "But if a drug dealer shoots someone right in front of them, they don't see it." Another galling double standard: cop-haters in the community rush to take down squad-car license plates when the cops are pursuing a vehicle. "How about taking the plates of drive-bys?" suggests Reedy.

Surely the cops would get more support from the community if their moral authority were not constantly under siege from left-wing activists both within and outside of police departments. Lieutenant Eric Adams of the NYPD has made a media career for himself by testifying against the department before every camera he can find, as the self-appointed head of a shadowy organization called One Hundred Blacks in Law Enforcement Who Care. Every time Adams says something negative about the police, observes Wilbur Chapman, the NYPD's Chief of Patrol during the 1990s, the department loses blacks who are "on the fence," whether as witnesses or potential recruits. "There's no voice to say: 'This is not the reality,'" laments Chapman.

The sum total of these pressures is a police force fighting with one hand tied behind its back, according to many black officers, contrary to black activists who incessantly portray police forces as out of control. Black cops, no less than white cops, support assertive policing. "You can't pull your gun, no Mace—why don't we just arm-wrestle to see if you go to jail?" asks Detective McLaughlin. Reedy chimes in mockingly: "The liberals are crying that 'crime is up, rape is up.'" Nods McLaughlin: "If they let cops be aggressive and do the job, we'd get a handle on it."

Sadly, the media and politicians never recognize these moderate voices as valid representatives of black officers. The perverse logic of race politics, even within police departments, dictates that the only authentic blacks are angry blacks. And so the "spokesmen" for black officers are almost always the most radical members of a department, usually unelected, who push a grievance agenda of quotas and lower standards.

Baltimore's department, like that of Washington, D.C., suffers from a particularly virulent form of internal race politics. A very small but vocal group of black officers is playing the race card against the white commissioner, Ed Norris. Lieutenant Barksdale could not be more disgusted. "I have no time for the-white-versus-the-black mentality," he scoffs. "Where were the radicals when 261 black kids were getting killed a year? It didn't matter to them, because we had a black commissioner. This commissioner has dropped homicide levels to their lowest in a decade. [In 2000, homicides dropped below 300—to 261—for the first time in ten years.] I'm sick of [the politics]." Barksdale argues that when the radicals claim discrimination in assignments and promotions, they are merely deflecting attention away from their own shortcomings. "If you asked them, 'What have you done on this job?' you'd find excessive medical history and excessive complaints against them.

Some cops don't deserve the uniform; they're scared to do the job they swore to do."

As with the racial profiling charge, being black does not immunize managers from charges of racism. Bridgeport chief Wilbur Chapman is struggling with his own radical clique of officers. "I have people who talk 'black,'" he says, "griping that 'African Americans don't get this or that'—and all that other crap. When it's time for them to step up to the plate, they're not there." The NYPD's black Guardians Association harangued Chapman, when he was New York's Chief of Patrol, for not having "enough" blacks on his staff. "I looked to see who could do the job best," he says unapologetically. "Right now, I'm 68 officers short. I want 68 of the best officers I can get. I don't give a damn what color or sex they are."

Racial bean-counting reached its zenith in the 1970s and 1980s, when federal courts across the country imposed on police departments draconian quota systems for hiring and promotions and threw out meritocratic standards. Chicago was enjoined from looking at a recruit's arrest history; Akron couldn't consider school discipline, academic records, or neighborhood references. In 1980 a federal judge ordered that one-third of the NYPD's recruits be black. To move things along he lowered the passing score on the entrance exam for blacks to 84, ten points lower than the requisite score for white recruits.

William Hubbard remembers that era in the NYPD, and deplores it. "They decreased the standards for promotion in 1976: all the passing scores were lowered for minorities," he recalls angrily. "It was an injustice to all those blacks who had succeeded without decreased standards. You accepted the argument that you were inferior." Hubbard rejects the idea that the promotion test was biased. "If you just studied, instead of going out on Saturday night and having fun, you could have passed it."

Alleged racism in promotions is a favorite topic of radical cops and anti-cop agitators. In its crudely ignorant post-Diallo report, the U.S. Civil Rights Commission accused the NYPD in 2000 of discriminating against would-be minority commanders; Eric Adams preposterously resurrected the same charge against the NYPD's current commissioner, Ray Kelly, just three months into his term of office.

In fact, as is always the case in such charges, the discrimination runs in exactly the opposite direction. For every position to which promotion is discretionary, rather than determined by an objective exam, blacks and Hispanics in the NYPD jump the queue at a breathtaking rate. They become detectives almost five years earlier than whites, for example; whites wait twice as long to be appointed to deputy inspector or deputy chief as blacks and Hispanics. If such a disparity showed up in whites' favor, it would be attributed to racial discrimination, not merit.

The most destructive quota pressures come in the area of discipline. Radical officer organizations forever allege that disparate rates of discipline reflect managerial bias, not actual misbehavior, and they are ever ready with individual and class-action lawsuits to put teeth in their claims. In February 2002, for example, a divided jury awarded $1.72 million to an Akron police officer who claimed he had been fired because of his race—not because he had broken his wife's jaw. The Philadelphia Guardians Association is currently collecting data on discipline rates by race; in 1999 the Clinton Justice Department notified the Dallas Police Department that it was under investigation for its disciplining of black officers. As a result of such actions, managers think long and hard before taking necessary disciplinary measures. Ed Flynn, chief of the Arlington County, Virginia, police force, says that he will extend a longer probationary period to a "non-thug" black cop with discipline problems than to a similarly situated white cop. "I want a paper trail that says you got more breaks rather than fewer," Flynn admits. Naturally, white cops resent this double standard.

Baltimore's Barksdale sees this disciplinary hesitation all the time and rues its consequences: "You have to fire bad officers, because they will screw up. It cripples the department."

Actual analysis belies the racist punishment charge. In response to a still-pending lawsuit by the Latino Officers Association, the NYPD analyzed its disciplinary records several years ago and found that black and Hispanic officers were indeed punished at higher rates, but only for those infractions that carry mandatory discipline, such as drug use or criminal behavior. Black male officers failed drug tests four times as often as white male officers, for example, and they received mandatory discipline for off-duty misconduct like assault and grand larceny nearly three times as often as white officers. Any discretionary punishment, on the other hand, was carefully meted out in exact racial and ethnic proportions. It's unlikely that officers are more careful about following rules in matters for which punishment is discretionary and thus uncertain. Assuming that rates of rule-breaking are constant between mandatory and discretionary disciplinary categories, blacks and Hispanics are therefore underdisciplined whenever managers have the leeway to do so.

The long-running race racket that has so distorted our national discourse shows no signs of letting up, but that is only because we have been listening to the wrong people. For every Al Sharpton or Eric Adams, there is at least one Carl McLaughlin or Tony Barksdale who speaks of American opportunity and fairness. There is no inherent reason why only the victimologists should be granted legitimacy as representatives of black interests, especially since so few of them are elected. Why not at least give equal time to a Wilbur Chapman, say, when he argues that the "biggest impediment to minority advancement is white guilt" and asserts that, whatever the remaining problems in American race relations, "the bottom line is: no one can stop me from getting my piece of the American dream"?

As for the state of policing itself, while my interlocutors don't constitute a perfectly constructed randomized sample, neither do

Eric Adams and his counterparts across the country. And, unlike the cop-complainers, these pro-police cops are not seeking benefits or power from their testimony. I believe that the support for law enforcement expressed by these officers is widespread among black policemen. Their voices represent an essential, and wholly overlooked, perspective on current law-enforcement controversies, one that should give us hope not just about the politics of policing but about race relations writ large.

"Let's Lock People Up!"

DETECTIVE CARL MCLAUGHLIN keeps popping out of his chair during an afternoon's interview. Perhaps that restlessness explains why this large detective with an elastic smile is the highest-producing gumshoe in his station house. "I'm relentless," he explains, pacing in scuffed-up jeans. "I never stop."

McLaughlin is a shining example of how the best in policing today is exuberantly color-blind. McLaughlin's mentor was the late Jack Maple, the flamboyant mastermind of the NYPD's Compstat revolution. The homburg-topped bon vivant spotted the future detective when both were in the Transit Police. Maple offered McLaughlin an undercover job in his pioneering decoy squad—the "path to destruction," as Maple ironically put it. The young cop figured he was ready for the crazy hours and danger, but he was not prepared for the magnitude of New York's seamiest side. "I had never seen so much crime in my life," he recalls. "I was shocked." When he transferred to Flatbush's 67th Precinct, he says, "I felt like I was in a candy store. In Transit, most of the crime is transient. Here, every other complaint had the same name on it."

McLaughlin proceeded to clean up. In his first year in the 67th, he made 179 arrests, more than twice as many as the next-highest-achieving detective. His productivity peeved the regulars.

His buddy, Detective Robert Reedy, also a new arrival from Transit and the runner-up in the arrest contest, warned the grumblers that if they told McLaughlin to slow down, he'd just work twice as hard. "This job is fun—how could you not like this job?" he grins. "They could put up a tent, sell it as a circus."

McLaughlin's energy was infectious. "He pulled me along," Reedy acknowledges. "He said: 'Get a car. Let's lock people up!'" When McLaughlin made second-grade detective, arrests shot up all over the Brooklyn South Command, as others sought to follow his lead.

Like many of his colleagues, McLaughlin came from a strict home but had his own brush with the law growing up. Approaching a subway turnstile, he thought, "I can pay and not have pizza, or jump and have pizza." His conscience lost. After the cops yelled at him for two hours in the station house, his father took him home and tanned his hide. "From then on, I said, 'It's not worth it.'" He entered the Police Academy in 1984 at age twenty at his mother's urging. It was a rough transition after the laxness of college. Yet by then he was hooked.

His work ethic helped him get through September 11. "Giuliani said, 'You should live your life,' so two days later I went and arrested someone," he recalls. But policing will never be the same, he and his buddies lament. For the first time they are scared. Unlike petty thieves and hustlers, he says, "the terrorists are willing to die for their cause. You know what? A person like that you can't stop."

For the moment, though, McLaughlin is still laughing at the job, even at the internal race politics. "[Commissioner] Kelly could appoint a black woman, a gay Chinese woman, a gay man, and there'll be someone who's mad because there's no midgets. He can't win," McLaughlin jokes. As for his own attitude on race relations? "I love everyone."

2002

America's Best Urban Police Force

I'M ON WHAT I THINK is a routine ride-along in Flatbush with Officers Peter Morales and John Ferretti, when the police radio crackles: "Shots fired at 3102 Foster Ave." As we screech to a halt in front of a big red apartment complex, Morales and Ferretti rush into the building and run up to the roof. "Police, don't move," they yell at a man scuttling down the fire escape. He dives into a sixth-floor apartment and empties his .357 Magnum out the window at the pursuing Morales. As the shots ping off the metal near him, Morales holds his fire: he doesn't have a clear shot that wouldn't endanger civilians. "I'm being fired on," he screams into his radio. Sirens blaring, a battalion of cars and vans roars up; cops of every description spill out; a helicopter buzzes overhead.

Inside, accused drug dealer Ricki Elam, twenty-seven, throws his gun into the oven and runs into his aunt's apartment next door, police allege, surprising her with a man friend. Elam rips off his do-rag and shirt, the cops later tell me, revealing a different-colored shirt below, and tries to sneak away in the commotion. But the cops coming up the stairs recognize him despite the costume change and collar him. The charges: attempted murder of a police officer, burglary, illegal gun possession—on top of his already pending drug charges and a gun charge.

This is a typical police story that you'll never find in the New York press. Capturing a gun-wielding felon without firing a shot—as police have done 155 times since 1995—doesn't fit the orthodox profile of a trigger-happy police force. Nor will New Yorkers ever hear about the collaboration between residents of this Brooklyn building and their local precinct to drive dope dealers out of the complex, or about the vocal support for cops I heard in the neighborhood. These facts contradict the preferred narrative of an isolated, racially biased force that scorns community involvement.

The press—led by the *New York Times*—along with criminologists, law professors, and activists, most of whom have never bothered studying the NYPD, has spun a distorted, error-ridden revisionist history of New York's crime revolution. Its harm extends well beyond New York, giving anti-police activists elsewhere ammunition to oppose the Gotham-style reforms that are any city's best hope for reducing crime. The basic story—which I've cobbled together here from Fox Butterfield's annual anti-NYPD article in the *New York Times*, other *Times* articles, a recent Jeffrey Rosen *New Republic* piece, stories in the *Los Angeles Times* and the *Economist*, and conversations with various academics—goes like this:

In the pre-Giuliani Golden Age, Mayor David Dinkins inaugurated "early and successful experiments in community policing" (Butterfield), which Mayor Giuliani mysteriously junked in favor of brute force. Giuliani's NYPD simply "thr[e]w people at the problems" (Butterfield) rather than think strategically about problem solving. Other cities' police departments reached out to the clergy, listened to the community to learn its concerns, and made "citizens the allies of the police" (Butterfield). Not the NYPD.

The Giuliani-NYPD strategy centered on the tiny undercover Street Crime Unit, which Butterfield and Rosen think is Giuliani's creation, though it dates from the 1970s. The unit stops and frisks vast numbers of innocent people, declare the revisionists, hoping to net an occasional illegal gun or fugitive. By contrast, other departments require their "officers to have a reasonable suspicion before stopping a subject" (the *Economist*). Meanwhile the rest of the NYPD enforces a mindless "zero tolerance" policy regarding petty crime and quality-of-life offenses. Officers and precinct commanders have lost all "discretion" regarding where and when to enforce the law (Rosen)—though, even so, they concentrate discriminatorily on minorities (Rosen).

The results: the bullet-ridden bodies of Amadou Diallo, an innocent Guinean immigrant killed by the Street Crime Unit outside his Bronx apartment on February 4, 1999, and Patrick Dorismond, an innocent Haitian shot by an undercover narcotics officer during a midtown altercation on March 16, 2000. When not actually shooting unarmed citizens, the NYPD has been creating a legacy of "fear" (Butterfield), evidenced in spiraling civilian complaints.

Almost nothing in this account is accurate. Let's deconstruct it and get to the truth:

Myth 1: Community policing was successful under Mayor Dinkins and his commissioner, Lee Brown.

With almost as many definitions of "community policing" as there are police forces, hardly a department in the country doesn't claim to be doing it. But the core ideas are: an attention to local conditions, especially quality-of-life problems, rather than just the big felonies; an effort to solve the underlying causes of particular problems; working with local residents and with other government agencies to respond to crime and disorder. In the public's mind, community policing also taps nostalgia for the tough but friendly beat cop who knew everyone in the neighborhood and kept them in line with a sharp word.

Under Mayor Dinkins, Commissioner Lee Brown aimed to flood New York with highly visible beat cops who would be local problem solvers, community organizers, and liaisons to other agencies. In reality, poorly trained young foot patrolmen wandered aimlessly over their territory, without knowing what they were supposed to be doing. "The only clear thing about the mission in those days was the beat book," recalls Patrick Harnett, then division commander in the Bronx. Officers abandoned their beats to waste two hours a day in the station house, recording the community meetings they attended and community contacts they made that day. The area each cop was supposed to cover was so vast that some neighborhoods never saw their community-policing officer at all. The cops themselves often joined the program because they could set their own schedule—which somehow always ended up 8:00 to 5:00, Monday through Friday.

Commanders in the city's highest-crime neighborhoods soon saw that Brown's community-policing idea was simply the wrong program at the wrong time. "There were 2,200 homicides a year, and cops were devoting hours to cleaning up junkyards," recalls former chief of department Louis Anemone, then a Bronx division commander. "It was sad." Says Harnett: "Brown's community policing used the social worker model at a time when Rome was burning."

Myth 2: The NYPD junked community policing and started merely "throwing officers" at crime.

If a key component of community policing is problem solving, New York's internationally heralded Compstat process, developed by Anemone and Jack Maple in 1994, is the most refined community-policing program around, in sharp contrast with Commissioner Brown's unfocused efforts. The twice-weekly Compstat meetings, in which top department brass grill precinct commanders about crime in their precincts with the aid of computerized crime maps, are nothing other than high-pressure problem-solving sessions. In them, for the first time, the department's chiefs and local commanders began sharing information and bringing all the department's intellectual resources to bear on problems. "People were amazed at the resulting creativity," recalls the Kennedy School of Government's Frank Hartman, who was a consultant to the NYPD at the time. "Arrests were not the criterion, but rather: have you solved the problem?" By the end of 1994, district attorneys, U.S. attorneys, probation and parole officers, and federal agents were attending Compstat meetings to share information and coordinate crime fighting.

Giuliani's first police commissioner, William Bratton, reproduces a typical Jack Maple Compstat interrogation in his book *Turnaround*: "I want to know why those shootings are still happening in that housing project! What have we done to stop it? Did we hand out fliers to everybody? . . . Did we run a warrant check on every address at every project, and did we relentlessly pursue those individuals? . . . What are we doing with parole violators? Of the 964 people on parole in the 75th Precinct, do we know the different administrative restrictions on each one, so when we interview them we can hold it over their heads? And if not, why?" While the NYPD's critics praise other cities' departments for such things as targeted warrant checks, parole crackdowns, and interagency collaboration, New York's innovations led the field in just those areas.

Far from "throwing people at problems," the NYPD used Compstat to target its resources with pinpoint accuracy—even building by building. Commanders could direct quality-of-life enforcement at shooting hot spots, knowing they'd pick up gun toters that way. With similar strategic thinking, Bratton directed officers to pursue all accomplices in gun crimes, to seek out suppliers, and to ask all arrestees where to get guns in the city. Police had estimated that there were as many as two million illegal guns in New York when Bratton took command, but by August 1995 the proportion of arrested suspects toting guns was 39 percent lower than in 1993 because people were afraid to carry.

The results were unprecedented—anywhere. Crime dropped 12 percent in 1994, compared with 1.1 percent in the rest of the country. Homicides fell 19.8 percent, compared with 5 percent nationally. For each of the next six years, crime continued its free fall.

Remarkably, NYPD critics object that Compstat is not real "problem solving." According to naysayer Rana Sampson, a police consultant in San Diego and an inevitable Fox Butterfield source, Compstat policing relies on police "bodies," not "brains." Its analytic time frame is too short. Real problem solving, Sampson and others say, corrects the underlying environmental conditions that lead to crime, rather than simply enforcing the way to public safety.

The ideal type of problem solving that such critics envision would have been wildly irrelevant for 1990s New York. Emeritus law professor Herman Goldstein, the original theorist of "problem-oriented policing" and another frequent Butterfield source, describes a typical problem-solving project he is overseeing: a "very penetrating academic study" of thefts from vehicles in parking structures in Charlottesville, Virginia (population: forty thousand, the size of the NYPD; homicides in 1998: one). For each parking facility he is making an "in-depth study of physical design, the quality of the fencing, lighting, whether there are attendants on duty, and whether they are paid." To do the study well will take a "long time." Eventually Goldstein hopes to establish whether, for example, the highest-risk facilities are less well fenced. Then, he says, "we can play around with altering the conditions to decrease the theft."

New York's problems could not wait for "penetrating academic studies." As Jack Maple replied when accused of being too adversarial in the Compstat sessions: "I don't have time to be nice." I asked Goldstein whether facing several thousand murders a year creates a sense of urgency that cannot afford lengthy academic studies. And with gun violence, for example, what is there to study other than precisely what Compstat targeted: the sources of illegal guns, the networks of suppliers and users? "New York is entirely different," Goldstein admits. "With violent crime, the primary need can be police expertise, but you still need community members to come forward." Too bad he didn't tell Fox Butterfield that.

Though dedicated to problem solving, Bratton explicitly rejected the idea that the beat cop should be the main neighborhood problem solver. No green recruit could take on the problems of a complex Gotham neighborhood, he said. Bratton's problem solvers were the savvy, experienced precinct commanders, whom he unflaggingly held accountable for results. He also discarded the promise of a cop on every block, instead concentrating patrolmen on commercial avenues and at transportation hubs, where crime actually happened.

Finally, he rejected the standard rhetoric of the community partnering with the police to solve crime, at least violent crime. Bratton's policing—and that of his successor, Howard Safir—is unapologetically expert-driven. The citizen's role is to provide information to the cops, help set priorities, and obey the rules—though the police do have continuous contacts with their constituents. But New York never created a formal apparatus of citywide citizen crime-solving meetings, as have other cities. "If your crime problem is big and violent," says Northwestern University political science professor Wesley Skogan, the nation's foremost academic expert in community policing, "citizens should stay home." Citizens are "good at clean-up," he says, such as nuisance abatement and beautification. But for coming up with tactics to take out a drug gang, that's for the police.

Myth 3: The New York police are not involved with the community.

Try telling that to residents of a Model Block in Far Rockaway—part of a high-intensity police program to push criminals out of some of the most crime- and drug-ridden blocks in the city. I asked a group of Model Block mothers how they would change the NYPD. Blank silence. Then one woman volunteered: "We don't have no problems. The police respond immediately. They listen immediately to community concerns." Do these mothers read the reports of police harassment? "Every day; but thank God, where I live, we don't have it," the same woman answered. "I don't believe the reports," another said. "They want attention, that's the way I see it." What about Al Sharpton? "Al Sharpton doesn't speak for us," a third said. "He doesn't come to Far Rockaway. Our precinct is more like family than a precinct; our officers spend more time in the community than at home."

In precincts throughout the city, commanding officers attend community and church meetings almost daily. Says Jean-Pierre Louis, who runs an umbrella organization of Haitian community groups and churches in Flatbush: "The police are definitely willing to listen at a local level. We don't have any problem." Father Joseph Weber, pastor of the Holy Innocents Church in the 70th Precinct, where Abner Louima was assaulted, says that "churches in Flatbush have an active positive relation with their precincts. The commanders are very sensitive to our needs. But that is not what most people want to hear," he adds sardonically.

In the 77th Precinct in Crown Heights, where two and a half days of violent rioting occurred under Mayor Dinkins, cops reach out to kids, taking them roller-skating, coaching them, attending youth meetings and talent shows, and opening up the precinct's computers to children after school. Many officers spend Christmas giving out toys to hospitalized kids. In the Bronx's 43rd Precinct (where Amadou Diallo was shot), Detective Elliot Parisi can't stop talking about the teens he mentors in the Boy Scouts. "I can't begin to express how much those kids mean to me," he tells me. "You gotta see the beauty in these kids' hearts."

Though the department doesn't trumpet the rhetoric of community problem solving, community-police collaborations happen all the time. In a typical operation the 67th Precinct's commander, Deputy Inspector Harry Wedin, is working with "all the good people who want to take back" the building where Officer Morales was shot at on my ride-along. He urged the landlord to post "No Trespassing" signs throughout the complex, which cops enforce vigorously. He deputized residents to call in drug activity. Undercover officers were mapping the building's entire drug operation until an officer was shot. Too "enforcement-oriented," as community-policing purists would charge? What is the department supposed to do? Cops can't "reengineer" a massive, seventy-year-old apartment complex to "reduce opportunities" for dealing; they can't spend months studying lighting or fencing when the real problem is an infestation of criminals.

None of these local interactions gets reported, because the New York press almost never covers precincts—which is where the most positive police-community work occurs—unless something goes dreadfully wrong. The one time in recent memory that the *New York Times* wrote about a positive precinct event, it inoculated it with a strong dose of hatred toward the police.

In June 1999 the paper made it out to the 71st Precinct's fifth annual community picnic, featuring pony rides, cops flipping hamburgers, and lots of warm feelings toward the police. That is not, however, how the paper chose either to open or to end the story. Instead, after briefly and ironically presenting the scene through the eyes of the precinct commander ("a world that looked sunny and fine"), the *Times* gave voice to a sour onlooker, Gordon Franklin, thirty-two, a road manager for the rap group Gangstarr. "It's propaganda," he spits out angrily.

Now what is Gangstarr? The *Times* doesn't say, but it is a group known for its anti-white lyrics. Its former lead singer, "GURU," once broke a beer bottle on a woman's head, smacked her in the face, held her at gunpoint, wounded and bleeding, and refused to drive her to the hospital. Reason: she had pointed out his hypocrisy in dating white women while bashing whites in his songs. One might guess that Franklin shares his group's racial outlook, since he immediately invokes Louis Farrakhan: how would the police be behaving, he asks accusingly, "if this were a Louis Farrakhan event?"

Only after getting Franklin's perspective do we hear from the picnic participants, who swear that police-community relations are much improved in Crown Heights since the 1991 riots. Just so the reader doesn't come away with the wrong impression, the *Times* makes sure to end the article with Franklin. Pointing his finger at the white precinct commander, who is standing nearby with his back turned, Franklin blurts out "in a moment of bitter anger": "You know, my feeling is I'd knock him out."

Now maybe Franklin is a fine, upstanding member of the community, who hates the police because they have so abused innocent him. More likely he represents a breed of professional cop-haters who profit from fomenting more hatred of the police. For the *Times*, however, he is a valid barometer of community opinion, and his is the message that lingers.

Could the police do more outreach? Of course. And the more they do, the more goodwill they will create. But they also have to maintain public safety. After all, in the Lee Brown era, a Bronx borough chief remembers, "cops were shaking everyone's hand but not getting anything accomplished."

Myth 4: The NYPD has created a "climate of fear."

It is a staple of NYPD reporting that people now fear the police more than criminals. Without any effort I found examples aplenty of the opposite.

Natasha, a petite twenty-year-old with long dark hair tumbling out of a head scarf, watches the police cordon off the building where Ricki Elam allegedly shot at Officer Morales. "They say cops are bad, but they put their lives on the line," she says decisively. "They're not here to harass you; they're here to protect you. Ordinary people don't help you like that." Three boys walk past; one snarls "bastards" in the direction of some officers nearby. "He needs to get his little ass into school," Natasha retorts.

It's the criminals who worry her, not the cops. "This whole complex is filled with bad people," she says, "people who sell guns to teenagers, dealers in each building who have thirteen-year-olds buying drugs for them. I've seen everything." When Natasha observes a crime, she calls the police. "I could get killed for that," she reflects.

Round-cheeked Robert, thirteen, was on his way to get a haircut with his little sister when the shooting started. He seconds Natasha's views. "We can't wait to get out of here; it's too scary." Do the police harass you? I ask. "I think it's good that they stop people," says Robert, an Explorer Scout. "The police should be stricter."

There is a huge reservoir of support for the NYPD, as easily accessible to a reporter as the hostility that alone gets covered. Even some people caught up in the enforcement system are good-natured about the police. Vladimir Lamarre is sitting on a bench in Brooklyn's 67th Precinct waiting to speak to a detective; a "lady" had accused him of bad-mouthing her in Creole. What does he think about the police? "They're all right," says the twenty-five-year-old city parks worker. "Once you don't do any trouble, you don't get any problem." Do they treat you politely? "Yeah."

The point is, one could as easily write an NYPD story filled with people like Natasha as one filled with people like Gangstarr's Gordon Franklin. Which would be correct? Polls suggest that there are more Natashas out there than Gordon Franklins, and that—until the Louima, Diallo, and Dorismond incidents—support for the NYPD was rising under the Giuliani-Bratton regime. In the spring of 1996 an Empire State survey found that 73 percent of New Yorkers had a positive view of police, compared with 37 percent in June 1992. By 1998 a federal Bureau of Justice Statistics survey showed 84 percent of New Yorkers age sixteen and older satisfied with the police, including a surprisingly high 77 percent of black New Yorkers. But most New Yorkers experience the police primarily through the press, and for the last year or more the press has relentlessly told them only one story.

Plenty of anti-cop sentiment existed before the Giuliani era, of course, and when Bratton-Safir policing actually began enforcing the law vigorously, some people came to dislike the police more intensely, as family members or neighbors were arrested. Fanned by the Al Sharpton–*New York Times* winds, their anti-police feelings burned all the hotter.

And neighborhoods of people who feel this way make the NYPD's job harder. "Last Saturday night, a twenty-three-year-old boy was shot and killed," a squad commander in Brooklyn tells me bitterly, by way of illustration. "His friends were with him; everyone knows who killed him. The only person who cared was the mother. I asked her to tell his friends to come and help solve the murder. She asked them, but they refused—his best friends. So I try to find them. One takes off, running. I'm chasing the kid, and people are blocking me. If the community really cared, I'd solve every murder. The community's only 'the community' when they want to trash the police. I attend every wake, I embrace every victim of crime, do whatever I can to solve the pain, and the rest of the community stays away. No one cares." Sums up crime strategist Jack Maple: "If we could get 'the community' to press charges and show up in court, we'd be batting a home run."

Myth 5: Quality-of-life enforcement is discriminatory.

In a remarkably misinformed *New Republic* cover story last April, George Washington University law professor Jeffrey Rosen suggests that quality-of-life enforcement discriminates against minorities, because poverty forces them to conduct more of their life, including vice, outdoors. He should listen to Luz, from 139th Street in Harlem. The police enforce a lower standard of community civility above 110th Street, where Harlem begins, than below, she complains. "Sometimes the struggle is: do the police take quality-of-life issues seriously enough?" she says. "Let's say someone wants to barbecue in the middle of Broadway. The police's attitude is: 'Maybe it's legal.'"

A bleeding heart like Rosen would argue that of course it should be legal. Where else will these poor outdoor chefs go? Luz's attitude is: they're encroaching on our common public space, blowing smoke in our windows; cart them off. There are no more insistent advocates of order-maintenance policing than the law-abiding residents of dangerous neighborhoods like Luz. And there are many thousands of them.

Community-policing theorists insist that cops must understand how intensely citizens care about the raucous kids or intimidating beggars on their own corner—more even than about felony reduction. But Giuliani's NYPD needed no coaching on that front. One of its earliest crime strategies, "Reclaiming the Public Spaces of New York," targeted "street prostitution, aggressive panhandlers, sales of alcohol to minors, graffiti vandalism, public urination, unlicensed peddlers, reckless bicyclists, and earsplitting noise churned out by 'boom box' cars, loud motorcycles, clubs, and spontaneous street parties." When it comes to responding to community priorities—the keystone of community policing—the NYPD was way ahead of the game.

Myth 6: The Street Crime Unit and "stopping and frisking" are the very essence of Giuliani's NYPD.

Talk to the architects of New York's anti-crime revolution and the Street Crime Unit never comes up. Nor does stopping and frisking. Yet this tiny unit—less than 1 percent of the city's force—has become the centerpiece of the revisionist history because four of its members shot Amadou Diallo. And the revisionists portray stopping and frisking as the NYPD's main (and illegitimate) weapon against crime.

In fact the essence of Giuliani crime-busting is the unprecedented gathering of crime intelligence through the Compstat process, the rigorous follow-up, and the accountability for commanders. It is debriefing all suspects about any unsolved crimes and investigating every shooting as seriously as a murder. It is interagency cooperation. To be sure, officers are instructed to question people stopped for minor offenses, and to arrest and search parole violators, repeat offenders, and wanted persons. This too is part of modern policing's intelligence-gathering strategy.

Cops report that in 1998 they did 138,887 stop-and-frisks, 85 percent of them on blacks and Hispanics—less than the 89 percent of suspects identified as black and Hispanic by victims. Assuming that police stopped mostly young men, and that they stopped everybody just once, that would mean that they stopped 11.6 percent of all minority males between ten and forty-five. But press reports insist again and again that the police are stopping the same people numerous, even dozens of times. Assuming, very conservatively, three stop-and-frisks per person, that amounts to 3.8 percent of this group—hardly a rampage, and less than the 6 percent of young men that criminologists estimate commit much of the city's crime. The press specializes in blissfully ignorant innuendos about stop-and-frisks to tar the NYPD. In a 1999 article unfavorably comparing the NYPD with the Boston Police Department, the *Economist* pointed out portentously that after 1989 Boston required its police to have a "reasonable suspicion" before stopping a suspect. Implication: New York has no such requirement. Well, if Boston waited until 1989 to promulgate that rule, it was sure getting lousy legal advice. The "reasonable suspicion" requirement has been in place since 1968, thanks to a Supreme Court opinion justifying stop-and-frisks. New York follows that requirement no less than Boston.

Myth 7: Bratton-Safir–style policing encourages brutality.

Revisionists sounded this theme early. In April 1995 David Dinkins absurdly complained to *Newsday* that Bratton and Giuliani "seem to care more about 'kicking ass' than increasing the peace." New York University law professor Paul Chevigny opined to the *Los Angeles Times* late in 1995 that Giuliani's crime-fighting strategies contain the seeds of police violence. "The military analogy leads to brutality. The military is brutal," he warned darkly.

Here are the facts. Complaints of excessive police force have plunged since former mayor Ed Koch's time, though Koch is now a full-throated member of the anti-NYPD chorus. In 1984 citizens lodged one excessive-force complaint per every seven officers; in 1995 one per every ten; in 1999 one per every nineteen.

The actual use of force has followed an identical pattern. The number of intentional shootings by the police dropped more than 50 percent from 1993 to 1999—while the department grew nearly 40 percent. Fatal shootings by police officers in 1999—eleven— were at the lowest level since 1973. Compare that number with the nine fatal shootings in 1999 by San Diego's 2,064 sworn officers—a whopping rate of nearly 5 per 1,000 cops. The rate of fatal shootings per 1,000 officers in New York is .28, compared with .96 in Chicago—home of the most extensive community-policing experiment in the country; 1.14 in Washington, D.C.; and 1.68 in Houston, presided over by Mayor Lee Brown, New York mayor Dinkins's former police commissioner.

To be sure, overall civilian complaints against the police rose in 1994 and 1995, as Giuliani increased the force by 23.6 percent and directed it to start enforcing the law vigorously. But from 1995 to 1999, civilian complaints per officer declined 22 percent, and they went down over 10 percent more in the first four months of 2000. The department's incessant training in civilian relations seems to be paying off.

Early in the Bratton regime, Chief Patrick Kelleher built up the relatively toothless Internal Affairs Bureau, tasked with rooting out police corruption and brutality, into the most elite of all the NYPD's departments. Giuliani's and Safir's response to the Louima torture—basically cleaning out an entire precinct—was unprecedented in its harshness and swiftness. Bratton publicly humiliated members of the 30th Precinct found to have stolen from victims and suspects. Safir has fired more officers for misconduct than the previous two commissioners combined. Two tragic shootings over six years and one undisputed act of brutality hardly show a force out of control. All departments make mistakes, usually without such relentless criticism as has engulfed the NYPD; but then, those departments are not headed by a mayor who is anathema to the liberal establishment.

Myth 8: New York could have solved its crime and community-relations problems by modeling itself on other departments.

If only we had policed like —— (insert your favorite city), lament the revisionists, we could have achieved our extraordinary crime drops without police killings and community friction. No city is too small, none has a demographic or a crime profile too wildly dissimilar from New York's, to serve as an accusatory foil. The *Times*'s Butterfield ludicrously holds up Fort Wayne, Indiana— population: 200,000, a little larger than a large New York City precinct—as a useful model. Fort Wayne, he tells us, divided itself into 227 neighborhoods, each with a liaison officer to other city agencies. Following that model would require dividing New York, absurdly, into 8,286 community-policing neighborhoods. Fort Wayne cut murders by 50 percent from 1994 to 1998, says Butterfield sharply, but incorrectly. Actually it lowered homicides 36 percent, from 38 in 1994 to 24 in 1998. Well, New York lowered murders 59 percent, from 1,561 to 633.

The comparisons always supposedly show that "community policing" fueled these other departments' success. Somehow community-policing failures never get trumpeted. Take Chicago, whose community-policing program, the country's most long-standing, Butterfield improbably puts forth as a "thriving" model. In fact Chicago has done a lackluster job of both crime reduction and community relations. While New York cut its crime rate 44 percent from 1994 to 1999, Chicago reduced its crime rate just 18.6 percent. New York decreased murders 65 percent from 1990 to 1997, compared with Chicago's 10 percent. The crime rate per capita remains 225 percent higher in Chicago than in New York; with half Gotham's population, the Windy City has about the same number of murders annually.

Whereas 84 percent of New Yorkers aged sixteen and older were satisfied with the police in 1998, only 80 percent of Chicagoans were. More black New Yorkers (77 percent) than black Chicagoans (69 percent) approved of the police. Police shootings produce the same charges of rampant racism in Chicago as in New York.

Getting Chicagoans to show up at beat meetings, wherein the community and the police are supposed to solve problems jointly, remains a continuing challenge. Even Mayor Richard Daley, who inaugurated community policing with great fanfare in 1993, no longer seems so enthusiastic about it. As a Chicago lieutenant, quoted by Northwestern's Wes Skogan, put it, "The spark has gone out."

Baltimore is an even more cautionary community-policing flop. Ex–police commissioner Thomas Frazier used to brag that his force was the only gang in town that could save a child, run a recreation center, and get an addict into treatment, according to the *Baltimore Sun*. He had assigned eighty-eight officers to the indisputably worthy Police Athletic League but only five to tracking down the fifty thousand suspects loose on arrest warrants. He effectively decriminalized drug possession.

The results? Baltimore's per capita homicide rate, fourth in the nation in 1999, was seven times the national average and five times New York's. Baltimore ranked first nationally in robbery, fourth in assault, and tenth in rape. Its cops shot civilians at four times the rate of New York's officers. Drug dealers had become so shameless that they refused to move when asked by a police officer.

Martin O'Malley won the mayoralty in this predominantly black city last year by promising zero tolerance for crime. He brought in New York's Jack Maple to sketch out the sort of smart, information-based policing that drove down Gotham's crime, and he recently tapped Edward Norris, the NYPD's deputy commissioner for operations, as commissioner. Thanks to the constant misinformation about New York–style policing in the New York and national press, Norris faces a public relations struggle to give Baltimore the policing it needs.

Chicago and Baltimore are not rare exceptions. A 1994 study of eleven community-policing experiments found a mere 50 percent success rate. Worse, as of 1997, only one of the eleven projects had survived. Political scientist Skogan cautions that the limited scope of documented evidence so far makes community policing vulnerable to the charge that "it is mostly a public-relations triumph."

Instead of ever mentioning places like these, NYPD-bashers usually cite San Diego and Boston to disparage New York. Like New York, these cities have had astounding and comparable crime drops since the 1990s, and they vie with Gotham for first place nationally, depending when you start counting and what you measure. The *Times*'s Butterfield picks 1991 to 1998, when the murder rate dropped 76.4 percent in San Diego, 70.6 percent in New York, and 69.3 percent in Boston. Measure from 1990, however, and New York's 72 percent murder-rate drop edges out San Diego's 71 percent, while Boston tops both, at 75 percent. Measure from 1994, Giuliani's first year in office, to 1999—and look at all FBI index crimes, not just homicide—and New York leads not just all three but all big cities, with a 44 percent crime-rate drop. San Diego is in third place nationally at 38.6 percent and Boston in fourth place at 34.5 percent. Even after the reduction, though, Boston's crime rate remains 40 percent higher than New York's.

Clearly all three cities deserve enormous credit. But where did they start from? In 1993, the year before Giuliani took office, San Diego, with a murder rate a mere two-fifths that of New York, had 133 killings; Boston, with a murder rate two-thirds that of New York, had 98 killings. New York had 1,946. New York was facing a much larger problem. Bringing down nearly 2,000 murders 67 percent, as New York did through 1998, requires preventing 1,313 homicides (not to mention all the lives saved in the intervening years), 14 times as many as the 91 homicides San Diego fended off to bring its murders down to 42 in 1998.

The people most closely involved in the three cities' successes scoff at comparing them. "This is why I get aggravated with criminologists and reporters like Butterfield," says William Bratton, hardly a defender of New York's current policing. "They do reports from each other." As Boston's police commissioner, Bratton began that city's community-policing efforts before Giuliani recruited him to head the NYPD. "We did things very differently in Boston, because it is a different city. As for San Diego, it has nowhere near the density of New York. It's not teeming with people. It has a different population mix and a higher income level."

San Diego has embraced the Goldsteinian problem-solving method to great effect. Working with residents, beat officers analyze the preconditions of crime, above all property crime, and try to prevent recurrence. But this mostly nonminority, affluent, beachside paradise, with a population 16 percent that of New York's, has never had a serious crime problem. It has never had gun violence to speak of, says Al Guaderrema of the San Diego Police's Crime Prevention Unit. And it has benefited enormously from the Border Patrol's crackdown on the San Diego–Mexico border over the last several years. San Diego's "most difficult crime situation in the last eight years has been thefts from autos and auto thefts," he says—a far cry from New York's gorgeous mosaic of felonies. "What works in San Diego wouldn't work in New York," says John Welter, San Diego's assistant chief of policy and planning. "Broken windows needed addressing in New York," he says, but not in San Diego, which has never had that degree of street disorder. Similarly, San Diego could come the closest of any big city to driving authority and discretion down to the beat-cop level because its force is a manageable two thousand men, not Gotham's forty thousand. (Nevertheless, recall that San Diego police fatally shoot civilians at fifteen times the rate of the NYPD.)

Boston is another great success story but also one of difficult application to New York, say its prime architects. "The cities are in completely different scales," observes Captain Robert Dunford, who heads a precinct in the Dorchester neighborhood. With 550,000 people, Boston is half the size of San Diego and less than one-quarter the size of Brooklyn. And its own leaders are quick to acknowledge the NYPD's accomplishments. "New York was an exemplar in the Bratton era," says Jim Jordan, the Boston Police Department's director of strategic planning. "We learned accountability from New York."

In the early 1990s Boston's chief crime problem was highly

specific: youth gangs were shooting each other up, mostly in three small neighborhoods with a combined adult population of 104,000. Police estimated that only 150 to 250 kids were committing most of the city's violent crime.

The Boston cops, therefore, could develop a sharply focused strategy. In partnership with federal prosecutors, they gave gang members an ultimatum: use a gun, even just get caught with one bullet, and you're doing federal time—big. Taking a cue from New York, the police directed quality-of-life enforcement at the gangs. And most famously, the police and a small group of minority ministers—the Ten-Point Coalition, led by the charismatic Eugene Rivers—began collaborating on preventing youth violence. Teams of police and ministers visited schools and homes sending the message: stay out of trouble or pay the price.

Attend a Wednesday morning meeting of the Ten-Point Coalition at the elegant olive Victorian house where Eugene Rivers conducts his street-savvy youth ministry, and you'll hear statements that make you think you're in another universe from New York. Coalition member Reverend Larry Mays is presiding, and cops, probation officers, and officials of the schools and social work agencies are in attendance. The meeting focuses on a recent surge in youth violence. "The two pillars of the drop in youth violence are the preachers and the police," Mays observes. "The third pillar— the parents—is really frustrating." Mays's statement is typical of Ten-Point candor. Adds Rivers: "There's certain things the police and the mayor can't say [about personal responsibility]; the community has to say it. But the community is in denial."

The ministers, however, have no problem saying those things, loudly and often. The Coalition is currently under attack for a flyer it distributed in the violent Cape Verdean African community: Attention Cape Verdean Youth! You bring the noise, you get the noise. Welcome to America. "The Boston police said: 'Count us out, this is too provocative,'" laughs Ten-Point member Mark Scott. Rivers once announced at a middle school: "The Bloods and the Crips will be crushed." Had the police made such a statement, denunciations would have thundered down.

So cordial is the relation between the ministers and the police that the ministers sing the cops' praises: "When the police do the right thing, you have to do everything you can to make sure it gets coverage," pastor Ray Hammond of the Bethel AME Church tells me. And so great is the trust between the two groups that the ministers point out the worst young malefactors to the police, while, on the ministers' say-so, the police go easy on first-time offenders whom the ministers volunteer to straighten out themselves.

The NYPD actively cultivates relations with the minority clergy too, but it has yet to find any ministers willing to take as public a position on personal responsibility as those in Boston. "The major difference between New York and Boston's black leadership is the willingness to address black-on-black crime," explains Eugene Rivers. To the Boston ministers, the moral cowardice of New York's black leaders is obvious; only New Yorkers don't see it. "I have no comment on Al Sharpton," says Reverend Mark Scott acerbically. "But it erodes one's moral authority when it is blatantly obvious that crime is a problem—that most people being shot are not shot by cops—and you're silent on the issue."

University of Pennsylvania criminologist John DiIulio, under the auspices of the Manhattan Institute, tried to found a New York Ten-Point Coalition, without success. "No New York ministers wanted to get involved," he says tersely. Commissioner Howard Safir has asked clergy to talk about black-on-black crime and to acknowledge that the real danger in poor neighborhoods comes not from cops—"but every time I'm called a racist," he says. Perhaps Safir is the wrong person to raise these issues, but critics who use Boston as a cudgel to beat the NYPD should suggest a list of leaders who are prepared to ask the hard questions about family responsibility and youth violence. The police would undoubtedly love to work with them.

This isn't to say that Boston has solved the problem of race and policing. Complaining about harassment for "driving while black" is a "standard routine" for blacks during traffic stops, says traffic officer Kenny Gee. And in a park just down the street from the Dorchester police station, you can hear plenty of Gordon Franklinesque hostility toward the police. "The majority are total garbage, just garbage," says John, a thirty-two-year-old public works employee who sports a big, gold pistol charm around his neck. John is probably no more reliable a judge of policing than Gangstarr's Gordon Franklin; the New York press, however, would treat him as an expert.

And for all the fanfare around Boston's police-clergy collaboration, Boston's civilian complaint rate—used by the *Economist* as a cudgel against New York—is virtually indistinguishable from New York's: 1 complaint per 7.7 officers in Boston in 1999, compared with 1 complaint per 8 officers in New York.

San Diego has its share of racial tensions too. Last August, San Diego cops fatally shot a former NFL player, Demetrius DuBose. The subsequent grandstanding would be familiar to any New Yorker. "The Urban League joins the rest of the African-American community in denouncing the legal lynching of another African-American citizen," said president John W. Johnson. "When will the killings of our black sisters and brothers cease?" The head of the Black Contractors Association, Abdur-Rahim Hameed, suggested that "African-Americans would be better off shooting it out than being shot down in cold blood." Last February, after the San Diego police killed a homeless man, participants in a community forum claimed that black kids were growing up scared of police—a charge that would make any New Yorker feel right at home.

Yet in San Diego, as in Boston, there are also voices of moderation that are all too rare in New York. A black San Diego councilman, George Stevens, publicly rejected the charges that Demetrius DuBose was "lynched." "There's not one piece of evidence that these officers shot Mr. DuBose because he's black," he told a community meeting. No New York black leader said anything comparable after Amadou Diallo was shot.

NYPD brass are well aware of the criticism that they should police more like other cities' departments. But many top New York cops have reservations about those cities' highly touted strategies. They think that Boston, for example, came perilously close to a "deal with the devil," in Louis Anemone's words, in singling out gun violence as the one infraction that would bring down the full weight of the law. They wonder whether the message was: we'll regard anything short of gun violence more leniently. There's some evidence this could be so. A prominent youth-outreach worker who helped forge Boston's approach to youth violence told a Kennedy School researcher: "I'm not even going to talk to a kid about stopping selling drugs until I can get him a job." He went on to laud the Boston police for "overlook[ing] a lot of people on purpose, because they weren't violent criminals. They stuck to their word, . . . and that showed a lot of respect."

It is that kind of relativizing—"how can you ask a kid to stop selling drugs when there are no jobs out there?"—that worries New York cops. Boston police captains brag about their jobs programs and other social programs as much as about their enforcement strategies. Their department has unquestionably embraced more of a social services approach to youth crime than the NYPD has, and it always presents its tough message of law enforcement in conjunction with an offer of social services. Since 1996 the department has distributed more than $2.2 million in federal funds to community groups, a surefire way of gaining support.

In a world of mushy terminology, it is refreshing to find some clear disagreements. "We're a little resistant to the Boston model, because we don't think we need it," says Gary McCarthy, the NYPD's deputy commissioner for operations. "I'm skeptical of social services, because I've seen the effect of enforcement. Social services won't stop people from wanting to make the quick buck.

People are lazy. What does work is when you lock a person up, he's not committing any more robberies."

McCarthy is no knee-jerk hard-liner. He is a hero in Washington Heights for creating the city's first Model Block on 163rd Street, the hub of the East Coast drug trade in the early 1990s. After taking out an entire local drug operation, McCarthy and his officers formed tenant associations in each building and worked with the community to clean up the block and "instill civic pride," he says. The results have been spectacular: in 1992 the 34th Precinct set a city record for homicides, with 120; last year the area had 8. "It was like the sun came out," recalls McCarthy. "I saw a 12-year-old trying to ride a bike for the first time in his life, because he had never been allowed out before."

So McCarthy is hardly averse to working with the community, but he doesn't believe in offering social services or a government-funded job as a quid pro quo for not committing crime. The Model Block is not a social services program; it simply helps people take responsibility for their neighborhood.

After so much relentless criticism, the NYPD is in crisis. Demoralization, especially in the Bronx, is dangerously high. "Cops have to be believers," says a Bronx borough commander. "It doesn't get any worse than the Bronx district attorney comparing the Diallo shooting with a drive-by shooting. The officers are afraid to engage the bad guys, knowing that they might become the bad guys." A patrolman remarks: "Knowing what I do now, I'd never take this job again. I love the job, but you get all the racist abuse. You're always wrong."

The price of such demoralization is steep. A plainclothes officer in Brooklyn gives the street perspective. "This place is getting busy again," he says. "Guns are back on the street, because guys know they won't get tossed." In the Bronx, homicides are up 60 percent this year. And the mauling of women after the Puerto Rican Day parade this June gave New Yorkers a brutal refresher course in order-maintenance policing: when, fearful of racism charges, the cops back away from enforcing the law on the so-called small things—public drinking, drug use, defacement of property, litter—the chaos that lurks beneath the surface of this huge metropolis can explode.

To combat the revisionists, Mayor Giuliani and Commissioner Safir should throw open the department, now bunkered in and defensive, calling in the press and community leaders to see Compstat sessions and precinct-community programs, and showing off the Police Academy's innovative training programs. By the same token, they should make straightforward acknowledgments on those occasions when cops make serious mistakes. But the longer the revisionists continue their crusade against the police, the further New York's crime-fighting legacy is likely to erode.

"Journalism 101"

WANT TO BE A STAR REPORTER for the *New York Times*? Worried about the pressure to come up with new material? Don't worry! Follow the Fox Butterfield method of journalism and cut new research to a minimum. Simply recycle your material annually, sprinkle on a few new errors each year, and quote experts unqualified to pass judgment on the subject.

For the last two years Fox Butterfield, the *Times*'s national crime reporter, has criticized the NYPD for not policing like other cities. On April 4, 1999, while New York was still convulsed with the *Times*-led Diallo frenzy, Butterfield announced that "New York City has grimly discovered there is a price for the tough law enforcement tactics that have led to its steep drop in crime: estrangement between police and citizens." New York's fatal error, he claimed, was in abandoning community policing. He proceeded to trot out a handful of cities—above all, San Diego—that he claimed had used community policing to achieve crime drops comparable with New York's while improving community relations.

Exactly eleven months later, during the controversy over the Patrick Dorismond police shooting, Butterfield dusted off last year's article and reran it. Oh sure, he added some new cities and exacerbated the error-ridden caricature of the NYPD, but the basic tale was the same:

1999, admiringly quoting San Diego police chief Jerry Sanders: "Our basic premise is: we don't have enough police officers to do it all, so we need community participation."

2000, quoting Chief Sanders again: "Our basic premise was, we didn't have enough police officers to do it all, so we needed the participation by the community."

1999: Sanders "measures progress as much by an annual survey of public satisfaction with the police as by the actual reduction in the crime rate. The most recent survey . . . showed approval at 89%, he said."

2000: "In addition to using crime figures, Mr. Sanders decided to measure his department's success with an annual survey of public satisfaction. The most recent one showed approval at 89%, he said."

1999: "Based on the ideas of residents themselves, the police divided the city into 99 neighborhoods, with a police team assigned to each."

2000: "After a series of meetings with citizens, the police divided the city into 99 neighborhoods, with a police team assigned to each."

1999. "San Diego has only 1.7 officers per 1,000 residents, compared with 5 per 1,000 in New York City."

2000: "San Diego has 1.7 officers per 1,000 residents, compared with 5 per 1,000 in New York City."

1999: "Another component in community policing is 1,200 volunteers, many of them retired people who receive police training, wear police-like uniforms, and drive around in official vehicles."

2000: "The city also recruited 1,200 volunteers, many of them retired. . . . [T]hey receive police training, wear police-like uniforms, and drive official vehicles."

Butterfield also has his favorite criminologists, some of whom have either total recall or a limited vocabulary:

1999: "Rana Sampson, a former police sergeant in the city, who is director of public safety for the University of San Diego, said: 'What NYPD did was throw people at the problems. You can't put a cop on every corner, and do you really want to live in a society with a cop on every corner?'"

2000: "Rana Sampson, a former police sergeant in New York who is director of public safety for the University of San Diego, said: 'What the NYPD did was throw people at the problem, putting cops on every corner, but who wants to live in a society like that?'"

Butterfield never got around to checking whether his good friend Sampson still worked at the University of San Diego in 2000; she didn't.

University of Wisconsin law professor emeritus Herman Goldstein also makes regular appearances. In 1999 Goldstein scolded Giuliani and Bratton for eliminating community policing and investing heavily in police operations. "This was almost coming full cycle back to the 1960s," he said, "to the idea that the police alone can fight crime." In 2000 he told Butterfield enigmatically that a "community gets the policing it deserves, or demands," a statement that would seem to put the "blame" for New York policing on New Yorkers themselves, rather than on the usual Butterfield villains: Giuliani, Bratton, and Safir. Yet Goldstein had harsh words for the leaders as well: "They tried to do all this too quickly without the investment of years of groundwork in refined training and supervision and discipline. Historically, this is a prescription for runaway police organizations."

Before addressing the fallacies in these experts' opinions, let's examine their qualifications for pronouncing so definitively on New York. I reached Goldstein in his home in Madison. What do you know of New York policing? I asked him. "Not much," he said frankly. "I'm not studying New York at all. I just know it from a distance." I wasn't sure I had heard correctly. You haven't studied the department? No, he hadn't. "I understand the complexity of these matters. To speak authoritatively, you need to know more." He hasn't been to New York at all to study it since Bratton took over.

Goldstein advocates something called problem-solving policing. Arguably, New York is now an exemplar of creative problem solving. Isn't Compstat a laser beam for problem solving? I asked. "It may well be that Compstat does problem solving, I don't know."

Isn't New York trying to address quality-of-life problems, just as Goldstein recommended in his 1990 book? "I'm not saying that New York is not doing something. I would never say that, because I don't know."

Hasn't Giuliani introduced innovative programs to bring down crime, like domestic violence prevention? Goldstein was getting peeved by now. "As I told you at the onset, I don't know what they're doing."

How then did he make such specific accusations against the NYPD, suggesting it was a "runaway" organization? "Did I say 'runaway organization'? I was speaking more generally in the *New York Times*," he explains.

Goldstein even disclaims the central thesis of the Butterfield articles: that one can compare cities on their policing. "It's impossible to compare cities," he says.

Yet it must be a hallmark of criminologists to speak authoritatively on matters they have never studied. For even as Goldstein was acknowledging his lack of knowledge of the NYPD, he continued the attack. "Broken windows became transformed into an aggressive form of policing under Giuliani," he said. "This occurred when they found out that turnstile jumpers had weapons." Now this happens to be the wildly ignorant thesis of Jeffrey Rosen's April 10 *New Republic* cover story. So the misinformation loop runs like this: criminologists borrow from journalists, who then borrow from them, ad infinitum, until they have created an impregnable wall of untruth.

Rana Sampson, who accuses the NYPD of merely "throwing people at the problem," shares Goldstein's liberating lack of knowledge. Butterfield identifies her as a former NYPD sergeant, without mentioning that she hasn't worked or lived in New York since the late 1980s. For the last seven years—the entire span of the Giuliani period—she has worked in San Diego, absorbing news accounts, no doubt, which make everyone an expert.

Now let's examine these experts' opinions. Rana Sampson criticizes the Giuliani NYPD for "putting cops on every corner." But "who wants to live in a society like that?" she asks. Everything about this proposition is wrong. Trying to put cops on every corner has been a hallmark of the city's allegedly less "aggressive" police eras. The first commissioner to promise a "Cop of the Block" was Patrick Murphy, Mayor John Lindsay's liberal police commissioner, who asked his cops to "rap with the people and make friends." Commissioner Lee Brown also declared that the beat cop was back, and inaugurated a "Cop's Block" program. Mayor David Dinkins started the increase in the size of the force by adding five thousand new officers.

Far from putting cops everywhere, Bratton did the opposite. He repudiated as unrealistic the promise of a cop on every block and concentrated his forces on trouble spots. But as for no one wanting "to live in a society with a cop on every corner," as Sampson claims, that is in fact the "community's" fondest desire. Go to any precinct community council meeting and the most frequent and insistent demand is for more, and more visible, police.

Sampson's charge that Bratton merely "threw officers at the problem" shows a complete ignorance of Compstat, which made policing rigorously intelligent and information-driven for the first time.

Goldstein accuses the NYPD of lacking "supervision and discipline" under Bratton. In fact, Bratton was probably the most innovative and successful manager in the department's history. He drove accountability through every corner of the organization. Says Goldstein: the department should have invested "years of groundwork in refined training" before doing "all this" (i.e., crime fighting). What was the city to do while the department spent years in "groundwork"? And what the NYPD started doing was enforcing the law, something the Police Academy supposedly trained the cops to do as raw recruits.

Butterfield adds his own howlers to the article. He accuses Bratton and Giuliani of creating the dread Street Crime Unit, whose mission he misleadingly describes as "stop[ping] large numbers of people in high-crime neighborhoods." In fact, Commissioner Patrick Murphy created the unit in the 1970s to protect cabdrivers and truckers from violence, precisely what the unit is doing today. But it is beneath Butterfield to double-check his prejudices.

Butterfield lauds other cities for "listening" to community concerns regarding quality-of-life issues; when the Giuliani administration takes up such issues, it's not "listening to the community," it's a "crackdown on petty crimes."

The "Why Can't New York Police More Like Fort Wayne?" complaint is not Butterfield's only annual theme. Butterfield is nothing if not efficient. In September 1997, in an article titled "Punitive Damages: Crime Keeps Falling But Prisons Keep on Filling," he asked the mind-bending riddle: If the crime rate keeps falling, "why is the number of inmates in prisons and jails around the nation still going up?" Over the next year, apparently no one at the *Times* was able to point out to Butterfield the obvious answer: that crime was falling in part because more people were serving more time. In August 1998 the same Butterfield puzzle appeared on page one: "Prison Population Growing Although Crime Rate Drops." Eight months later, in "Prison Nation," he pointed out the same insuperable paradox.

How to Train Cops

CRITICS OF THE New York Police Department have attacked its officer training as vehemently as they've excoriated the rest of the department. Because the Police Academy fails to appreciate "diversity," they complain, it graduates officers insensitive to "the community," uncontrolled in the use of force, and, in the slanderous formulation of the U.S. Civil Rights Commission, all too likely to "torture or kill people of color."

Obviously none of these hyperactive critics has ever set foot inside New York's Police Academy. Anyone who has done so, with just an ounce of good faith, would have to conclude that the NYPD has forged a training message as relentlessly focused on restraint and respect as anyone could hope for. Education at the Academy is a model of how to integrate rigorous tactical instruction with an unequivocal mandate of communication and service.

And, far from ignoring "diversity," the NYPD is—to its detriment—awash in the spurious "diversity" ideology. Capitulating to political pressure in the wake of the 1997 brutalization of Abner Louima and the 1999 shooting of Amadou Diallo, the department has devoted ever more instructional hours to moronic "anti-racism" training. In so doing it has imposed an irrelevant solution on a far more complex problem: teaching officers to respond appropriately to challenges to their authority. The Academy does tackle the critical issues of attitude and authority forthrightly; it would have more capacity to do so, however, without its useless investment in sensitivity reeducation.

The crown jewel of NYPD training is In-Tac, for "In-Service Tactical Training," a series of role-playing exercises on New York streets, designed to put officers through as accurate a simulation of real-life policing as possible. The exercises reproduce situations New York cops have actually confronted, sometimes fatally.

On a quiet street next to an army armory in upper Manhattan, four recruits are making a felony car stop—the most dangerous job police ever encounter. Cars confer an enormous advantage on violent criminals: they can kill, and they contain a wealth of hiding places for weapons. A green Chevy matching the description of a car used in two recent armed robberies has just driven by; the gunmen are presumably inside. The recruits stop their patrol car and command over the loudspeaker: "Pull over! Driver, put your hands out the window and on the roof of the car! Take your keys out of the ignition, and put them on the roof!"

The corpulent, mustachioed driver whines: "Officer, I'm late!" In the next moment the front-seat passenger bolts from the car, dropping a gun as he flees. The recruits let him go, as they have learned to do, in order never to separate from their partners.

"I want to know why I'm being stopped, officer," whines the driver again, looking back over his shoulder. "Look away from me, look the opposite way!" shouts a recruit. "Why, officer?" the driver whines. The four recruits are now standing in front of their car with their guns trained on him. "This is f—ing bulls—t," says the driver angrily. "Look away from me," commands the lead recruit. Another recruit shouts: "There's someone in the backseat!" A man who had been lying down in the back of the Chevy leaps out and shoots the recruits.

Fortunately, this time the perpetrators are played by police officers, and their guns aren't loaded. The recruits have just had a tough lesson in cover, the most important tactical strategy in policing. The first passenger ran from the car to lure the officers after him, thereby providing an easy target for the hidden gunman. The recruits responded properly by staying put, though they should have transmitted the runner's description over the radio. But they then left the cover of their car to approach the suspicious Chevy, making them vulnerable. They should have stayed behind cover, called for backup, and made the driver exit with his hands up, to be cuffed next to the patrol car. Ideally, armored personnel from emergency services could then approach the car at a wide angle to check the seats.

People often think of police tactics as sharpshooter ploys. The opposite is the case. Proper tactics frequently can eliminate the need for force altogether. The decisions an officer makes as he approaches a scene often determine the level of force he ends up having to use.

The NYPD's tactical mantra is "cover, concealment, and communication." The first two imperatives buy an officer time and protection to figure out the nature of the threat and the safest way of defusing it. The third imperative means: communicate with fellow officers, the suspect, and civilians. Failure of all three Cs resulted in the death of Amadou Diallo. The four street-crime officers too quickly left the cover of their cars to approach Diallo's apartment vestibule; they had no apparent plan of action. Once they believed he was pointing a gun at them, they were fully exposed and had no recourse but to "shoot back," as they mistakenly, tragically, believed they were doing.

Some of the other In-Tac scenarios the recruits practiced that evening involved immediate levels of threat comparable to the hidden gunman exercise. Four recruits confronted a seeming robbery in progress: the "perpetrator," it turned out, was really a plain-clothes street-crime cop frisking a suspect. When the street-crime officer put his gun on the ground—as the lead recruit, still uncertain of the "perp's" identity, had commanded him to do—the real perp grabbed it and shot the recruit. Another group of recruits are sent to a shooting outside a factory; the collapsing victim—a gang member, they later learn—pulls a gun from her jacket and pulls the trigger.

Other scenarios, however, call above all on officers' social skills to decipher and calm ambiguous situations, any one of which could in an instant turn dangerous. Among them:

• Students stopped a stolen car; its driver claimed to be its lawful owner. The officers frisked the driver, spread-eagled, while he shouted: "I went to John Jay [College of Criminal Justice], I know my rights, you cannot do this!" Turns out he was telling the truth: he had just recovered the car from the stolen-vehicles depot, but the department had failed to put the transaction into the computer. The challenge became how to mollify a very angry man. "Oh, you gotta be super-nice," suggested an eager-beaver recruit. "Maybe assist him getting back on the highway."

• Recruits walked into a hysterical dispute involving a woman and two men. As the novice officers eventually pieced together out of the swirl of emotions, a ne'er-do-well living with his sister had allegedly stolen $300 from her; to complicate matters, the siblings' older brother, also on the scene, was an off-duty cop.

"Where's my money?" screams the sister as the recruits arrive.

"He wants to be a big s—t, officer; he never pays the rent," announces the older brother. "He's disrespecting my sister with naked girls in the bathroom." The older brother shouts at his sibling: "Is this a wake-up call for you yet? You're not embarrassed by this?"

A recruit pulls the moocher away from his sister. "Oh, you're going to take my wallet, sir? I don't appreciate being pushed," shouts the alleged thief.

"You hear that? He says he's going to hit me!" calls out the older brother. "Lock him up, officer, do me a favor!" he adds.

"You're calling me a f—king idiot? You're a f—king idiot!" retorts the younger brother.

After the scene ends, the supervising sergeant asks: "We're not here to make fun of you, but who was in control?" The older brother, came back the answer. The sergeant offered some tactics for controlling disputes: put the complainants back-to-back so they can't see each other and so you can see your partner; use code words if you're going to arrest someone, so as not to provoke early opposition; and, above all, your first question, once you learn someone is a cop, should be: "Where's your weapon?"

• Other recruits tried to get an emotionally disturbed man who was out on the highway flapping his arms to get back into his sister's car.

• A solo officer was called to a loud argument between the owner of a bodega and rowdies playing football and drinking beer outside her store. "You're fine when we're spending money, Carol; what's the big deal, I can't play football?" threatens one. The rowdies surround the officer, shouting at him. "Call your lawyer, Tony," one guy says. "I know he needs a warrant." One tough hurls the football on the ground toward the officer and storms off.

The In-Tac lieutenant, Thomas Messer, advises the recruits afterward: "You cannot let your temper take you. They'll know if they can get to you; be very careful not to get hooked." Several years ago, he reminds them, "someone threw a football, and now an officer is in jail for murder" (referring to Officer Francis Livoti, who was alleged to have choked Anthony Baez to death in 1994 after Baez's football hit Livoti's car; Livoti was acquitted of homicide but convicted of federal civil rights violations).

To listen to police critics, you would think that officer training consists of constant exhortations to aggression. In fact the Academy incessantly preaches that "professional presence" and professional language are an officer's most important law-enforcement tools, not force or threats. State troopers are figures of awe for so flawlessly embodying "professional presence." Detective Tony Augusto, the most charismatic instructor I came across, asks a large lecture hall: "Who's ever been pulled over by a state trooper? What did he look like?" "Very professional," came the recruits' answer. Augusto agrees: "They're ready to rock and roll. Interesting, interesting. Let's take a look at that. Once the hat's on, you know they mean business. Do they walk to your car? No, they glide. You can almost hear the 'Left! Right!'" he intones like a drill sergeant. "I'm a cop, and I'm intimidated. What do you think his first words are? 'Good evening, sir.' If you're pulled over by New York City cops, you're not quite greeted the same way."

The Academy faces a delicate challenge: while it constantly urges empathetic communication with the community, it also needs to turn often shy civilians into officers who are not embarrassed to assert their authority. "We're New York City officers. Guess what will happen out there?" asks In-Tac instructor James Foiles, an intense, bronzed sergeant with a face as sharp as a razor blade. "Sanitation trucks will be going by, helicopters buzzing overhead. You will have to be loud and articulate. If you're timid, that's out. If you say,"—and here Foiles switches into a soft, mincing voice—"'Excuse me, sir, can you please put your hands on the wall?' no one will listen. Rather: 'Sir! Please put your hands up!'" he barks out.

Back at the Academy, four recruits are practicing a gun run (a response to a 911 call alleging an illegal gun). They weakly try to persuade the suspect to take his suspicious hand out of his pocket while the suspects' buddies swarm around, adding to the confusion. "Freeze!" bellows Lieutenant Grace Telesco, head of the Behavioral Sciences Department, to stop the scenario. "How do you get the man in the white shirt to get his hands out?" she asks the class—the most daunting question in police work. "The officers here are so laid back, I'd never comply," she snorts. "You have to command in such a way that you're scaring him to death. I know that we're always talking about communication, but to be assertive in this situation is not to be discourteous."

The most inspiring class I observed at the Academy brilliantly addressed this thorny problem of persuading people to obey justified commands. Since 1995 the Academy has taught "verbal judo," a set of verbal steps for talking people into compliance. Tony Augusto, with his long face, diamond ear stud, and hair that starts short on top and ends up curling over his collar, *Saturday Night Fever*–style, turns the lesson into an extraordinary exploration of how to police humanely.

Augusto's organizing theme is the distinction between the "asshole" and the "professional." The asshole officer confuses his ego with his role as enforcer of the law. "It's not about us," he admonishes the class, pacing the hall in a coffee-colored shirt, blue tie, and pleated trousers. "You are not the message. You put someone in handcuffs because they've broken the law, not because you're the police." Augusto puffs his chest out, rocks back and forth on the balls of his feet, and chuckles gloatingly in perfect asshole style: "'Cuz I'm the police! Heh, heh, heh.'" He continues severely: "That comes from those three letters I despise, 'EGO.' No one cares that you're the police. When your ego flares up, your power and influence will decrease."

Augusto provides examples aplenty of the "disease of assholism" that afflicts too many officers. "'Why am I here? Because your wife called me! Sit the f—k down!'" he shouts self-righteously, in imitation of an unprofessional officer on a domestic violence call. He winces and shakes his head. "Horrible, horrible. You'll have a fight on your hands if you tell a man to sit down in his own home."

The professional knows how to deflect verbal abuse without escalating a confrontation. "When someone comes up to you: 'Oh, go f—k yourself, officer, I ain't doin' s—t,' your response can't be, 'Oh, go f—k myself?!'" Augusto retorts menacingly. "When we got sworn in, we lost one constitutional right. Which one? Freedom of speech. Our mouths keep getting us in trouble."

The goal of policing, Augusto keeps reminding the class, is to generate voluntary compliance. Period. As long as someone does what you tell him to, give him the last word. Doing otherwise will lead to disaster. "Don't be surprised if you hear this on the street: 'I'll do it this time, man, but if you didn't have that shield, I'd kick your ass!'" Augusto is talking over his shoulder, gesticulating angrily, while walking toward the door in imitation of a resentful civilian. "Who wants to call him back?" he asks the class about his imaginary miscreant. "He complied with a bad what? A bad attitude. What do we want to key in on, attitude or behavior? His attitude can't hurt us. I've never been knocked on my butt by a man's attitude." Augusto goes into asshole mode again: " 'That man needs an attitude adjustment,' " he announces pompously. Severely now: "Remember that you can't change a man's attitude; you can't beat it out of him."

Seasoned cops don't like this teaching, Augusto says. He imitates an angry cop whose authority has been challenged: " 'Hey, you! You!' " he spits out, calling back the imaginary perp for a lesson. "Gentlemen, get that tough-guy thing out of your head. It will put you in jail."

Augusto's is more than a negative philosophy, however. He just as vigorously counsels affirmative respect, even for criminals. You'll have toughs in your neighborhood who think they're even tougher than they actually are, he tells the class. Treat them with respect. "You may have to slam someone down and put him in cuffs. That doesn't mean you have to strip him of his dignity. The people you lock up may save your ass one night, when your backup doesn't arrive."

How do you get voluntary compliance from a thug? "You'll use this," Augusto predicts: " 'Things can be done the easy way or the hard way; we prefer the easy way.' I can't tell you how many times I've said to a perp: 'Put your hands behind your back, act like a gentleman, and you'll be treated like a gentleman.' Remember, at any moment it can go south. Even though I'm acting like a gentleman, what's going on in my mind? Preparedness."

Augusto's most uplifting message would transform the NYPD if it were universally followed. "Bring your humanness to this job, bring your personality," he says. "Don't be afraid to greet people. People are scared to say hello to us," he laments, "because we usually just walk on by."

Professional presence and professional use of words won't always work, unfortunately. "Will we always get voluntary compliance?" Augusto queries. "No," the class pipes up. He continues philosophically as he walks the hall: "However, we will get compliance—yes, yes, we will; as long as we're within our legal rights. If you get physical," Augusto coolly advises, "I expect you to go fast, go hard, just push them into the system, and go from there."

Police critics who seem to believe that the job can be done without force would be horrified by the plainclothes class in "subject control." Paired off on tumbling mats, officers in gym clothes practice martial-arts tactics for taking down noncompliant suspects. "If he's fighting, grab his left arm," loudly orders Wilfredo Torres, a pit-bull-compact officer in a polo shirt. "Don't hit him in the triceps or back—it will only tick him off. Hit him in the elbow to cause pain. Push down on his arm with your forearm and pull up his wrist, then go into the hammerlock [the finishing technique for handcuffing a prone suspect]. You can't get him down nonchalantly; you need a little pain all the way down. And give loud, clear verbal commands: 'Down! Down! Down!'"

The Academy necessarily teaches force options all the way up what it calls the "compliance continuum" through deadly force. At the same time, however, it immerses recruits in the service ethic. Policing, it stresses constantly, is about serving people. Classes on various needy populations such as the handicapped are filled with a palpable sense of humanitarian mission. In a discussion on the elderly, instructor Kevin Parker warned the recruits that, because older people's routines are so predictable, "everyone is watching them"—sometimes with larcenous intent. "So who else should be watching?" he asked. As one, the recruits rang out: "We should!"

The NYPD has evolved a complete blueprint for courteous, professional policing. Instructors insist—more obsessively than the NYPD's critics—that officers get to know people on their beat and treat them considerately. Where problems arise, it is usually because someone has violated Augusto's verbal-judo philosophy. He has allowed his ego into the job or, as In-Tac's Lieutenant Messer put it, has gotten "hooked."

Had Justin Volpe obeyed verbal-judo mandates, he would not have taken a toilet plunger to Abner Louima. That incident was a textbook excessive-force case, triggered as it was by a challenge to an officer's authority. Louima had scuffled with Volpe and resisted arrest outside a Brooklyn nightclub; Volpe taught him the proverbial cop's lesson in the most grotesque way imaginable.

To prevent such atrocities, the NYPD needs to devote every discretionary training hour to communication and self-control. It needs to increase role-playing exercises across the range of situations officers confront, from violently hostile to sympathetic. Instead, in the wake of the Louima attack, the NYPD took a far more politically expedient course. It increased "diversity training," validating the NYPD-bashers' claim that the Louima case was a bias incident. The evidence showed otherwise. Volpe was engaged to a black woman; their families socialized enthusiastically. Told of Volpe's likely role in the Louima torture, Volpe's fiancée exclaimed to the *Daily News*: "Justin a racist? Impossible!" Another officer involved in the assault, Thomas Wiese, was also engaged to a black woman, who was the mother of his son. Rather than race, the Louima case was about something far more difficult to solve: officers who treat resistance as a personal affront.

Imposing the distorting prism of race on more complex problems is a national compulsion, however: so the NYPD adopted the misguided recommendations of a post-Louima mayoral task force on police-community relations. The task force called on the department, in cringe-inducing language, to create a "safe space" where students could acknowledge their prejudices and answer such pressing policing questions as "What is racism, sexism, anti-Semitism, and homophobia? What is the difference between prejudice/bias and racism? What is discrimination, oppression, privilege, stereotyping? And what is diversity?"

It wasn't as if the NYPD didn't already put officers into a "safe space" to discuss their racism. The department had created the first police diversity training in the country in the 1970s; in 1991 the then-head of the Police Academy, Elsie Scott, said that she would devote a "large chunk" of Academy training to diversity issues, since many recruits come from Staten Island (read: "white Staten Island") and therefore "have stereotypes about the communities, especially black and Hispanic communities, and . . . can't distinguish between potential victims and potential criminals."

The 1998 Louima task force scoffed at the Scott-created diversity materials. So current Academy director James O'Keefe brought in Grace Telesco, a police lieutenant and Ph.D. candidate in social work, to make sure that "cultural-sensitivity issues" would get even more emphasis—and in their most up-to-the-minute guise.

Friendly and refreshingly unguarded, with a tough edge when necessary, Telesco remade the "cultural-competence" track of the Behavioral Sciences Department (which also offers such critical courses as verbal judo) into a simulacrum of today's politicized, race-obsessed universities, even down to brandishing her own sexual orientation as if it were a job qualification. The always cash-strapped recruits are required to shell out $38 for *Race, Class, and Gender in the United States,* a collection of resentment-filled essays edited by radical feminist Paula Rothenberg. Therein they read about the globally catastrophic effects of America's racism ("pervasive in the U.S. culture to the point that it deeply affects all the local town folk and spills over, negatively influencing the fortunes of folk around the world"); America's oppression of Asian-Americans ("Whites would deny us our right to speak out against majority prejudice, particularly because it tarnishes their image of Asians as 'model' minorities"); and its capitalist cruelty toward the poor, women, unwed mothers, the homeless, homosexuals, Jews, and blacks. Such cruelty, suggests a Rothenberg essayist, exceeds anything imaginable in other countries, including China, Algeria, India, and Brazil.

The recruits spend hours discussing and watching films on racism, sexism, homophobia, transgendered communities, and discrimination against the poor. They study a chart listing the various "privileges" that certain oppressor groups enjoy, such as being able-bodied, young, wealthy, or male. Students then break up into small groups to figure out how they themselves oppress or suffer oppression. "It really clicks for them when they realize that they're not afforded privileges because of class," beams Telesco. In discussing white privilege, they often make such telltale disclaimers as " 'I'm not racist,' " all the while "making racist statements," she says.

I ask Telesco if the recruits also discuss black racism. She looks at me as if I have announced that I intend to fly out the window. "Of course there is no such thing as black racism," she replies, flabbergasted at my ignorance. As experts such as the lesbian feminist poet Audre Lord proclaim, she says, "racism is power and prejudice," so blacks by definition can't be racist. Tell that to Korean and Jewish store owners, Chinese delivery men, and Mexicans working in fast-food restaurants in Harlem—all of whom these recruits will be responsible for protecting once they get out on the street.

Telesco is fiercely proud of the "cultural-competence" curriculum. "This is radical stuff," she boasts, quite accurately. "This is about oppression: how there's an oppressor and an oppressed." She chafes at the fact that such left-wing critics of the police as WBAI radio and the U.S. Civil Rights Commission have not given the department credit for its "progressive" curriculum. From her point of view, she has every reason to be upset.

Like former Academy director Elsie Scott's diversity training, the cultural-competence curriculum assumes that recruits come into the department with deep-seated biases. To an eye less practiced in spotting racism and sexism, however, the recruits seem among the most well-meaning and unprejudiced people one could hope for. Unfailingly polite, they speak eagerly about their desire to help others. Their companies are models of racial harmony, with constant bear hugs and joking across race and sex lines. Race is not an issue, recruits told me (though that disclaimer of course would not satisfy expert racism-spotters like Telesco and Scott), and company diversity is a source of pride for members. "The most helpful diversity training in the Academy is having been thrown in with the other thirty-four members of my patrol," says a willowy and thoughtful recruit named Richard Aspinwall. "I've never started a class with people so friendly."

So good-natured are the recruits that they take the Academy's anti-racism onslaught without a peep of protest. If asked, they will ingenuously volunteer that it was "taught like we're at fault because of the way we're born," as one recruit put it. But the white-bashing did not create any long-standing animosities, they say, and the companies thereafter go back to their prior color-blind state.

Seasoned cops are not so docile. Anyone who has ever gagged at the inanities of diversity training should wrangle a seat in the Academy's annual cultural-sensitivity "in-service training" session for plainclothes cops. There, for maybe the only time in one's life, one may witness victims of diversity training with enough guts to fight back.

The plainclothes cultural-sensitivity course was born out of another of the NYPD's politically motivated misdiagnoses. After the Diallo shooting, the NYPD's critics blamed endemic police racism for the Diallo tragedy. They were wrong; the Diallo shooting represented bad tactics, period. But the department caved in to the critics' pressure and carved out an entire precious day for extra plainclothes training to accommodate yet another diversity class. Like the Louima-inspired revamping of the recruit curriculum, the cultural-sensitivity course is wildly irrelevant to the real problems of policing.

The Academy's sensitivity trainers play the time-tested diversity game of Gotcha: they require the hapless trainees to cough up cultural "stereotypes," then triumphantly point to the stereotypes they have elicited as evidence of cultural insensitivity. "Tell me about Italians," urged the trainer. On it went through New York's different ethnic groups. For a while, the cops played along ironically. Puerto Ricans? "Throw a great parade." "Love those hubcaps." Cubans? "Fit a lot of people in a small boat." Dominicans? "Like flags." Irish? "I don't know: white trash." What's the definition of white trash? "Trailer parks." There followed an agonizing discussion of whether New York City has trailer parks.

When the trainer asked for stereotypes about blacks, silence descended. Why is that? the trainer asked, disingenuously. No one volunteered an answer. Finally a few officers threw out: "all brothers"; "good basketball players"; "love that weed." Frustrated by the waning response to all her ethnic prompts, the trainer prodded: "C'mon, what are you guys saying about these people when you drive around?" Silence. "I'd rather you be out in the open; what scares me is when you're quiet," she pushed, with the compulsive demand for self-exposure typical of today's culture.

Showing far more wisdom than any diversity trainer ever manifests, a lieutenant suggested: "Things that come into the open create problems. The media is always putting microphones in people's faces, making problems for everyone."

Undaunted, the trainer offered some examples of American racism to get things going again. Street names in the Southwest, she said portentously (and inaccurately), are Anglo rather than Indian or Spanish. No one understood this subtle point. "What's wrong with that?" asked a cop innocently. Countered she: "Did John or Mary build that town?" A stocky, tattooed Puerto Rican in a head scarf bluntly replied: "It's now America."

Pay dirt! Isn't that racism? the trainer asked victoriously. The cops would have none of it. "No, racism's the opposite." "They're starting something new; the past is all over." Though most officers remain unapologetically committed to assimilation, the concept is too dangerous for the NYPD. Following the Louima incident, the Academy removed all references to assimilation in its cultural-diversity training materials.

It was time to return to the script. "Unfortunately, stereotypes are usually negative. Very few of you give me the good end of it," the trainer said sorrowfully. This was blatantly false. The officers had cheerfully been throwing out idiotic "good" and idiotic "bad" ethnic tags with exquisite impartiality. But no one objected to her mischaracterization, and she arrived at her goal: "How do these stereotypes affect us when on we're on patrol?"

The joking was over. In an instant the class became a microcosm of the debate about the police over the last two years—except this time the cops got to talk back.

"Stereotypes don't affect me at all; a person is a person," asserted an officer.

Unsatisfied, the trainer tried the next officer: "How do they affect you?"

"I treat all people the same."

"Oh, so you treat everyone equally? You don't think this guy might have a gun or drugs because of his appearance?" she said sarcastically.

A rail-thin young undercover from Transit tried a quid pro quo: I'll give you your prejudice, you give me our professionalism. "I know guys who are 110 percent prejudiced, but everyone's still treated equally."

"I'd like to think that's the way it is," the instructor said, her voice heavy with skepticism.

"You don't think that's the way it is?" said a lieutenant from Queens, with considerable heat. "I've been nineteen years on this job; I've never seen someone say, go get that 'X.'"

"I'm glad to hear that's the case."

A street-crime officer sought to break through the trainer's condescension. "You may go for dress, sex, age. If I'm looking for a perp, you're not looking for a guy in a suit. You stop someone because of what they're doing. You might find this is the nicest kid in the world. . . . I say 'kid'; that's my prejudice," he said self-consciously, aware that everyone was supposed to be confessing to sin. (He needn't have been so self-critical. Males between the ages of fourteen and twenty-four, less than 8 percent of the population, commit almost half the nation's murders; black males of the same age, less than 1 percent of the population, committed some 30 percent of the country's homicides in the 1990s.)

Here was something the diversity trainer could work with. "Stereotypes can be anything—dress, as you say, or age. You'll stop a kid out there, looking like the typical perp."

A young sergeant in a Jamaica anti-crime unit tried to clarify: "Not one of us stops a kid just because he's wearing baggy clothes. If you see him raise his belt, then you may stop him."

Ever ready to instruct these seasoned street cops in their jobs, the trainer said brightly: "You know what? There are perps out there in a suit and tie, blond, blue-eyed."

Exasperated, the anti-crime sergeant said: "We're talking about violent crime!"

This sort of hard-nosed realism was unacceptable. Finally a large, walrus-mustachioed sergeant from Astoria blurted out: "I'm sorry, Donna, this is killing me. This is the second time we've sat through this class. This has nothing to do with cultural diversity. This is an insurance policy, because the media is saying we're all racists."

Now all hell broke loose, as two years of frustration over the press's caricature of the police boiled over. "All we hear is that we're racially profiling. I can't stand the media. They're a bunch of lying pigs," spat out a black Brooklyn street-crime officer who had refused to participate in the earlier inanities. "If I stop five black people, am I racially profiling? But if a white officer stops them, now it's race profiling!" he scoffed. "People forget that some guys are actually committing crimes." He added for good measure: "Since we're all fascists, and we like to beat everyone, why don't they bring a force from some other country and let them patrol the streets?"

The anger flowed onto the Civilian Complaint Review Board,

which cops universally loathe as an increasingly politicized body staffed by ignorant twenty-one-year-olds. "Why don't the CCRB punks get thrown into the back of a patrol car, made to do verticals in housing projects, get trash thrown at them from roofs, and have people pull their wallets out fast at them to get them to react?" fumed another street-crime officer.

The trainer tried to contain the fury. "The public knows what you're going through," she said soothingly. "They have no idea. None!" shot back the bitter response.

The mustachioed sergeant from Astoria made a last effort to explain the police's perspective. "I've worked in every neighborhood in this city. My precinct is one of the most diverse. I don't look at people as black, green, orange, or red. You're either a good guy or a bad guy. If you're going to raise my suspicions, I'll act based on my level of suspicion."

The police are among the last groups in society willing to make this distinction between "good" and "bad" guys unapologetically and unambiguously. It is central to their worldview, tied up with their loathing of criminality and its effects on the law-abiding public. From their perspective, they are profiling "bad" guys, based on repeated observation. The public, however, sees only race.

Such exercises as the plainclothes cultural-sensitivity course are a colossal and outrageous waste of time. It cannot be overstated how scarce training time at the NYPD is. Taking officers off the street for any additional instruction always requires enormous justification, for it dilutes patrol strength. To spend those precious hours on childish identity politics bears a huge opportunity cost, for the time could be spent on instruction—above all, training in communication skills—that would actually improve officer performance. Tony Augusto's wonderful verbal-judo lecture, after all, was just that—a lecture. The recruits had little opportunity that morning to try the communication techniques he advocated. The force would benefit infinitely more if it devoted the hours wasted on dis-

cussing white privilege to role-playing exercises about how to sub-
due hostile civilians with words alone, a challenge officers confront
on a daily basis.

Academy director James O'Keefe, a broad-faced, savvy former
cop, defends the diversity nonsense by saying recruits inevitably
bring society's problems with them to the Academy, including
racism and sexism. This response sidesteps a more complicated and
pressing issue: the job pressures and peer culture that can turn the
most well-meaning officers into sullen discredits to the profession.
Reality, not racism, is the biggest challenge for the police.

The enthusiasm with which most recruits begin their training
wanes after only a few years on the streets. Police are lied to, be-
trayed, and cursed at by the people they are trying to help; they see
communities close ranks around criminals; they are called into
scenes of utter depravity. O'Keefe knows this full well. "There is a
very complex erosion of the human spirit that goes on in policing,"
he says. "Good people are exposed to bad things constantly. Officers start to ask whether the job is even doable."

That's why officers who started out with the best attitude
sometimes end up with the most civilian complaints against them,
observes Mike Caruso, a beloved precinct commander in Harlem
and the Bronx, now in the anti-corruption Internal Affairs Bureau.
They cared too much, he recalls, and couldn't accept failure. "'I
told you guys to leave this corner,'" they'll erupt angrily, provoking
retaliatory complaints from drug dealers resentful of the interfer-
ence. Add to street stress a hostile press and the perception of low
pay, and you have a recipe for exceedingly low morale, tinged with
the rage expressed in the plainclothes diversity course.

Each Academy class vows to avoid this cynicism and apathy.
As the new recruits lined up outside a store in Flatbush this spring
to pick up their uniforms, passersby shouted: "'All you white boys
go back to Long Island!'" and "'We don't need you here; f—k the
police!'" recalls Robert Coppola, an upbeat twenty-two-year-old.
"You just gotta laugh at it," he says amicably. It doesn't happen only

in minority neighborhoods: two days later, Coppola recounts, a couple of middle-aged businessmen on the Metro-North train told him, "'Oh, you're a cop? You should petition people to show you their hands, so you don't kill them.'" "I had to laugh," he smiles, shaking his head.

Coppola acknowledges that "some guys get a little disillusioned after a few years," but he tries not to listen to them. "I don't think I'll get that way," he asserts.

Making sure Coppola and others like him retain their positive attitude should be a top priority of police training, both in the Academy and throughout an officer's career. Director O'Keefe plans an excellent program to counter the corrosion of the streets: he will bring all officers back to the Academy at their fifth year for a week of retraining, including discussion groups on stress, alcoholism, and suicide. But he could accomplish much more with a yearly debriefing to help officers cope with the onslaught of negativity they receive. All hours currently spent on sensitivity training for in-service officers should be pooled to try to make annual debriefing possible. These sessions should acknowledge the one true race-related challenge in urban policing, discussion of which is now taboo: the vastly disproportionate representation of minorities among criminals. Every officer I have ever spoken to maintains the credo that the worst parts of the city house far more "good" people than "bad." The work required to hold on to that truth during constant enforcement activity should be frankly addressed.

The question of how to train policemen is where Plato begins his account of the ideal state in *The Republic*, the book with which Western political philosophy begins. Here in the real world, the NYPD, which inducts thousands more officers into the force each year than most departments in the country see in decades, has crafted an impressive practical answer to the question. Its instruction program includes the reality-based, hands-on training that is the best preparation for the split-second decision making officers face in the streets. In addition, its teachers hammer home the ideal of service and professionalism at every possible opportunity. As it works to improve its already fine training, the department should focus obsessively on increasing officers' communication skills. Those, and not the diversity training that insults officers' intelligence and experience, are the real keys to bringing the city closer to the Platonic ideal of enlightened policing.

2000

Keeping New York Safe from Terrorists

OVER THE LAST EIGHT YEARS the New York Police Department waged the most successful war on crime in the city's history. The NYPD conquered fear as well as crime, and in so doing sparked an economic boom and a civic rebirth that drew millions of visitors each year.

Now fear once again threatens to shut the city down. In less than two hours, the maniacs who destroyed the World Trade Center killed more than twice the number of people as were murdered in all of 1990 (2,245), the pinnacle of New York's homicide epidemic. The city's economy is reeling from the blow.

Closing the country's borders to potential terrorists is essential to prevent future attacks. But even were U.S. immigration policies immediately and sufficiently strengthened (a doubtful outcome), New York and the nation still face the likelihood of attacks from people already in the country.

Fortunately the tools the New York Police Department developed to fight street crime—above all, the intelligence and accountability mechanism known as Compstat—are tailor-made for combating terrorism. Applying them to America's new war, however, will require solving one of the most enduring problems in policing: turf jealousy, especially between the FBI and local law-enforcement agencies.

Ali, a wholesaler of counterfeit designer goods in Manhattan's Garment District, knows terrorism firsthand. Hezbollah—the Lebanese Muslim militia—killed Ali's brother in Lebanon in the early 1980s while burning down the family house. Ironically, Ali's business district is a vast money funnel for Hezbollah. His fellow counterfeiters, who sell knockoff Fendi handbags and Yves St. Laurent scarves from tiny rooms scrawled with Arabic graffiti above Broadway, collect funds for the cause back home.

The tall, long-lashed thirty-five-year-old sees similarities between his former country and his current working environment. The counterfeiters, many of whom also sell guns and drugs, have spotters on each corner looking for undercover cops; better outfitted with communication equipment than most New York drug gangs, the bootleggers can quickly close up shop and disappear when alerted to a possible raid. "These guys all grew up in war—they know how to operate," he says. "It's like a terrorist camp here, like a military base."

The NYPD's Intelligence Division discovered the terrorist funding stream in the 1990s when it was investigating Garment District counterfeiting. It took the information to the FBI with an offer to help the bureau shut down the terrorism connection.

Not a chance, said the FBI. Get off of our turf. In fact, stop going after counterfeiting rings entirely, since you may compromise our own investigations.

Now, the FBI was technically within its rights in brushing off the NYPD's offer of collaboration. The bureau oversees the Joint Terrorism Task Force (JTTF) in New York City, made up of federal, state, and local law-enforcement officers, which by agreement has exclusive jurisdiction over local terrorism investigations. But by so precipitously rejecting the NYPD's aid, the FBI cut itself off from the department's unparalleled manpower and expertise. "The best of the NYPD's best is the best in the country," observes Robert

Gianelli, former commanding officer of the department's Emergency Services Unit. NYPD's most seasoned detectives are unmatched in their ability to debrief suspects. Undoubtedly some of the crooks the department picked up for counterfeiting could have been "flipped" and turned into informants about terrorist financing. Other street criminals may also know something about the funding network.

Current and former members of the NYPD fear that the Garment District conflict may be a preview of how the investigations of the September 11 attack will unfold. These NYPD veterans warn that the FBI is cutting itself off from a vital source of intelligence and manpower in the fight against terrorism—local law enforcement. No one is closer to the communities that harbor terrorists than local police officers; no one has greater resources to track down leads. But the traditional lack of trust between the bureau and the local agencies has limited the required collaboration.

"I believe the life of the nation may depend" on federal-local cooperation, testified Edward T. Norris, Baltimore police commissioner and former NYPD deputy commissioner of operations, to a congressional subcommittee in early October. The FBI's failure to include local law enforcement in its terrorism efforts is putting the country at risk, he warned. "The rules of engagement for law enforcement [must] change forever," Norris asserted. "We all need each other if we as a nation are going to successfully counter threats that can come from virtually anywhere, at any time, in any form, including forms that could destroy whole cities."

Norris complained that the watch list distributed by the FBI to local police a week after the attack contained only names, with no other identifying information, such as descriptions, addresses, pictures, or places of employment—making it virtually useless as a detection tool. "I frankly do not understand this," he testified. "When someone commits a murder, rape, or robbery, you plaster his picture all over police stations and, whenever possible, in the media, to help locate that individual before he commits another crime. Now we're looking for the murderers of thousands who may become the murderers of thousands, even millions, more."

The FBI has also kept its new leads dangerously close to the vest. In the days after the World Trade Center collapse, thousands of tips poured into New York's Joint Terrorism Task Force, overwhelming its ability to track them down. Meanwhile many NYPD detectives who weren't members of the task force were desperate to pitch in but were kept "sitting on their hands," reports Daniel Oates, former chief of the NYPD's intelligence division, now chief of the Ann Arbor, Michigan, police department. Nationally the FBI had received more than 260,000 leads as of October 9. Given that the FBI has only 11,500 agents compared with nearly 650,000 local law-enforcement officers, Ed Norris asks, "Why aren't we all working together to find the people the FBI is looking for?"

Norris cites a tip regarding a suspicious vehicle that the Baltimore Gas and Electric Company gave the FBI following the September 11 attack. The FBI never told Norris's Baltimore cops. "What if the truck shows up at other locations?" he fumes. "We could track it down."

NYPD veterans are still haunted by their truncated investigation of Rabbi Meir Kahane's 1990 assassination, which could have picked up early warning signs of the 1993 World Trade Center bombing. The detective who searched the home of Kahane's murderer, El Sayed Al Nosair, brought back from Nosair's home four file cabinets filled with Arabic documents. He locked them up in the 17th Precinct at 4 a.m. one morning. When he returned four hours later, the file cabinets were gone. The FBI had taken possession. Three years later the bureau discovered that Nosair's documents, which it had never translated, anticipated the Trade Center attack.

"It was the same big lie," recalls Norris, who oversaw the Kahane inquiry. " 'You guys stay away from our case!' " Are you sure the NYPD would have translated the documents? I asked Norris. "Of course we would have," he retorted. "We had a murder investigation under way." Besides, Norris says, you didn't even need to translate the files to know they were suspicious—the cabinets contained photos of New York City landmarks and terrorist manuals.

Former NYPD intelligence chief Daniel Oates bristles when recalling the inscrutable security alerts he used to receive from the FBI's Joint Terrorism Task Force at 5 p.m. Friday afternoons. "I'd be getting these bullshit phone calls from the JTTF: 'We have a threat to the Empire State Building.' 'What can you tell me about it?' I'd ask. 'Nothing,' they'd say. Eventually they'd disclose that it was a bomb threat. 'What's the source of the threat?' 'We can't tell you.' And then they'd all go home. And I'm supposed to advise the commissioner what to do!" exclaims Oates, shaking his head. "Their culture has to change."

It was to solve similar turf problems that the NYPD's Deputy Commissioner for Operations Jack Maple and Chief of Department Louis Anemone created Compstat in 1994. Police precincts were keeping crime and arrest information from each other for fear of giving a rival commander an advantage. But crime could not be conquered without maximum intelligence sharing, Maple and Anemone understood. So they began biweekly strategy meetings with precinct commanders and top brass, in which all participants were required to share everything they knew. At one early meeting, sensing a commander's continuing reticence, Jack Maple asked incredulously: "Whom in this room don't we trust?"

Maple's insistence that law-enforcement commanders should be presumed equal and trustworthy partners in the fight against crime produced spectacular results. With information pooled and subjected to intense analysis and sophisticated computer mapping, previously unseen crime patterns emerged. Compstat participants forged strategies to crush problems before they became major. Within months, crime was plummeting.

Compstat had another purpose: accountability. If a commander had no plan for attacking a local crime problem—worse, if he was not even aware of the problem—grilling from top brass would expose his managerial failure. At the next meeting, if he had made no progress, there was no place to hide. For the first time in the department's history, police officials were held accountable for reducing crime rather than solving crimes after they had occurred.

The FBI's anti-terrorism efforts should be Compstated in every city where the bureau operates. Where a Joint Terrorism Task Force exists, the commanders of the agencies represented should meet on a biweekly basis to interrogate task-force members about the progress of their investigations. Where JTTFs don't exist, the FBI should assemble comparable meetings with all relevant agency heads. The new Fedstat meetings would have two purposes: to ensure that each ongoing investigation is being relentlessly and competently pursued, and to share intelligence. The only fail-safe defense against terrorism is information, but it must be made available to those who can best use it. In many cases, that will be local law enforcement.

What about security objections? Doesn't enlarging the circle of supervisors overseeing terrorist investigations increase the risk of leaks or tip-offs? While such intelligence-sharing meetings need to take great precautions to protect sources, the possibility of leaking by top law-enforcement officials is overblown, argues former chief Lou Anemone. "You need to be accountable," he insists. "Secrecy only covers up incompetency." Members of Congress are granted terrorist briefings upon request; the nation's police commanders have at least as much need for that information to keep their communities secure and are certainly far more aware of the possibly lethal consequences of security breaches than hothouse politicians. Requiring Fedstat participants to obtain security clearances would meet the security concerns. But in the past, complains ex–intelligence chief Oates, the FBI seemed reluctant even to begin the clearance process. Anemone recalls that New York's mayor Rudolph Giuliani was still waiting for a clearance years after requesting one.

Even a former FBI bigwig agrees that a Fedstat for terrorism makes sense. "The notion of bringing more people in to see if investigations are focused properly is appropriate," says Lewis Shiliro, the recent assistant director of the FBI's New York office. "We have to share information on a more real-time basis with any affected institution."

Once agency heads are meeting on a regular basis to monitor terrorist investigations, the information-gathering resources available would increase dramatically. The NYPD, for instance, could target enforcement activities on suspected terrorist groups and then apply the strategy that worked so well for street crime: treat every arrest as an opportunity to get information about other crimes. Though only one of the nineteen hijackers of September 11 is known to have a criminal record, their associates, as well as previous terrorists, have been involved in a range of illegal activities that are far more likely to bring them into contact with police officers than with the FBI.

There are numerous ways to draw on the local police without compromising security. The FBI should create a primer on terrorist cells for beat cops, to help them recognize terrorism-relevant tips or behavior. A beat officer could use the information without knowing anything about specific investigations. But he does need to know that terrorists operate just like common criminals—they case the scene of the crime ahead of time. The nineteen hijackers made repeat visits to the airports they departed from to find the soft spots. Terrorists seeking to blow up buildings may throw up a car hood outside the location to buy time for observation.

Even New York's Human Resources Administration—which has discovered ten thousand fugitive felons, including twelve murderers, on its welfare rolls since it began cross-checking recipients' fingerprints against a national database of outstanding warrants—should check recipients against Interpol terrorist data too. In this vein, food-stamp fraud by grocers in the Midwest has long been linked to funding terrorism; cops should check New York's food-stamp rackets for the same connection.

Enlisting local forces brings in personnel with years of experience working the streets where terrorists blend in. Though the FBI
has outstanding agents and offers excellent training, some young
agents assigned to major cases are remarkably inexperienced.
"When the FBI came to debrief our Garment District informants,"
recalls former chief Oates, "they sent some rube junior agent from
the Midwest to go up against very sophisticated New York street
criminals. Afterward our CIs [confidential informants] were laughing about it."

Ali, the Garment District counterfeiter, offers a street-level
take on the FBI investigation in his area. "There's a difference between bookwise and streetwise," he says. "Just because you have a
college degree doesn't mean you know what's going on." Ali claims
to have tried to help the FBI; he told them, he says, that he has
seen people make surveillance tapes of Broadway. "But they don't
take us seriously," he says angrily. "They say we don't have enough
evidence. But they should take everything into consideration."

Ali's frustration with the FBI's high threshold of proof paral-
lels the dilemma faced by some incisive FBI agents in Minnesota.
The agents had tried twice to get a computer search warrant on
Zacarias Moussaoui, now a suspected confederate of the nineteen
hijackers, in the weeks before September 11. Moussaoui had told a
Minnesota flight school that he only needed to know how to operate a jet in mid-flight, not how to take off or land, and he was already under investigation by French anti-terrorist agents. Yet the
FBI bureaucracy insisted that the evidence did not support a war
rant; only after September 11 did agents search his computer and
find downloaded information about crop-dusting aircraft. Had the
information gone into the intense analysis of Compstat, the outcome might have been different.

Ali has some advice for the FBI: get cracking! "They should
make a couple of arrests [in the Garment District], so people think
twice [about terrorist fund-raising]." Not all Middle Easterners are
bad, he says, "but a lot here are. There should be a cleanup of

everyone who's suspicious. The majority of people here are illegal; they should be out."

Attorney General John Ashcroft and FBI director Robert Mueller have reached a similar conclusion. In early October, Ashcroft and Mueller ordered bureau agents to act more quickly on intelligence. Rather than slowly building up a detailed legal case against terrorist suspects, they should take them into custody. "The investigative staff has to be made to understand that we're not trying to solve a crime now," a law-enforcement official told the *New York Times*. "Our Number One goal is prevention." Echoing frustrated police chiefs, the official called for a culture change in the FBI.

No longer willing to wait for a federal invitation, some police chiefs are initiating their own terrorist investigations. The Baltimore department called in all its confidential informants and asked what they knew about terrorism. A former drug dealer mentioned someone who was planning to crash the mainframe computer at Johns Hopkins University, a crucial research center for bioterrorism. The suspect, a Tunisian working for Johns Hopkins's management information systems, had an outstanding deportation order; the police handed him over to the INS and seized his computer.

Such catches are just the tip of the iceberg. Hundreds of thousands of illegal aliens in the country have overstayed their visas, overwhelming the capacity of the INS to track them down. Their names should be included in the National Crime Information Center, a database of outstanding warrants that traffic officers can check when they make a traffic stop or fill out an accident report. Terence Gainer, deputy chief of the Washington, D.C., police department, wants the FBI's terrorist suspects in there as well. "If the FBI is looking for one hundred people, we are going to have the most contact with them, but we don't get the intelligence information we need," Gainer laments.

Precinct commanders should step up their outreach efforts to mosques and other Islamic institutions. There are undoubtedly people in such institutions willing to come forward with information about terrorism, out of altruism or for cash; accordingly, the local police should increase their visibility and accessibility. Police should work to build up trust throughout Muslim neighborhoods, says Ed Flynn, chief of police in Arlington County, Virginia. "Someone may call you up and say: 'I don't feel right about these new tenants; they're paying all their debts in cash,'" Flynn observes.

Local undercover work in the community is essential too. A former NYPD intelligence detective suggests checking out the coffee shops on Brooklyn's Atlantic Avenue for possible sources of information. How do you know which shops? I asked him. "The ones where people dance in the streets when things happen overseas," he said. Just such a celebration broke out in Paterson, New Jersey, following the September 11 attack, but trying to get intelligence now from that community would be futile. "Everyone would be on a high state of alert," warns the detective. Ideally you'd have someone there for at least a year before you actually need him. "I had undercovers going places for no reason other than for people to see their face, so if things go crazy they wouldn't stir suspicion," he recalls.

Inevitably the old, misplaced outcry about "racial profiling" will dog rational anti-terrorist efforts. "Law enforcement has been so sensitized to this, you double-guess yourself all the time," acknowledges Washington deputy chief Terence Gainer. The racial profiling curse has already resulted in one tragic missed opportunity. A Maryland state trooper stopped one of the hijackers for speeding, according to Chief Norris. Several of the driver's characteristics heightened the trooper's suspicion: he couldn't say where he was going or answer other questions; he was driving a rental car without luggage; he was a Middle Easterner. Nevertheless the trooper merely gave the hijacker a ticket and let him go. The trooper's reasoning? He would be accused of racial profiling if he questioned or held the man further. In light of the ACLU's fierce, years-long campaign accusing the Maryland state police of racism, who can blame him?

This is no time to capitulate to political correctness. A heinous crime has occurred; we know the identities of some of the perpetrators. We are now looking for their co-conspirators. We know that they belong to fanatical Muslim sects overwhelmingly from the Middle East, who meticulously guard entrance to their cells. The likelihood of a Southern Baptist black or Lutheran from Minnesota belonging to a terrorist cell is virtually zero. Law enforcement—including airport security—is stretched too thin in this epic battle not to target its resources.

New York's private security professionals should be part of the intelligence-sharing network too. An organization uniting the police and private security chiefs already exists in New York City, but the information communicated between the two sectors needs to be more detailed. "No one's closer than these security guys," observes former chief Anemone. "The hotel industry creates incident reports. I want that information—why was the maid startled when she entered Muhammad's room? I want to send my suits over." Ideally, suspicious activity would be communicated nationally across the public and private security spectrum. Patrick Kelleher, former NYPD first deputy commissioner and now head of global security for Merrill Lynch, observes ruefully: "Some American Airlines uniforms were stolen six months ago; it would have been nice to know that."

Information sharing needs to go right to the top. Tom Ridge, head of the new federal Office of Homeland Security, should call together the heads of all forty-six federal agencies under his jurisdiction regularly to review the investigations in each agency's domain. This federal counterterrorism Compstat would grill the agents responsible for each investigation with relentless precision, making sure that each investigation is on target. At the moment, no mechanism exists to hold the federal agencies accountable for results and force them to share information.

The traditional firewalls between domestic and foreign intelligence must fall too, since terrorism respects no such bureaucratic boundaries. Had the CIA, FBI, and other agencies been sharing and rigorously analyzing their respective intelligence in a Compstat setting, an early warning of the September 11 hijackings may well have emerged. The fondness of suspected terrorists for flight schools may have been noticed and understood, especially after an abortive attempt by nonpilot hijackers to crash an Air France jet into the Eiffel Tower in 1994. Currently the FBI has refused to give U.S. consulates abroad access to its crime records, according to the *New York Times*—records that could be crucial in deciding whether to grant someone a visa. Attorney General John Ashcroft is trying to encourage the information sharing needed to stop terrorism, but Congress, out of knee-jerk civil libertarian zeal, is gutting his proposed legislation that would allow greater disclosure of wiretap information among federal agencies and would share grand jury information with national security and intelligence agencies.

To make the nation safer, policymakers also need to overhaul immigration rules and enforcement. The United States has had a de facto amnesty for immigration violators for years, and the official attitude toward immigration abuse has grown even more casual under President George W. Bush, who promised the Middle Eastern lobby during the campaign that he would ease up on deportations. In the future, visa applicants should be able to document a valid reason for entering the country, and federal authorities should make sure they leave when their visas expire.

Though immigration policy largely lies outside local control, New York City has only made a dangerously negligent situation worse. In 1989 then-mayor Ed Koch declared New York a sanctuary for illegal aliens, and every mayor since then has affirmed his policy. Koch forbade city workers from reporting illegal aliens to the Immigration and Naturalization Service. Though his executive order made an exception for crime, in practice even alien arrestees rarely get turned in to the INS. The estimated 400,000 illegal aliens in the city exist outside any official tracking system—until, that is, they end up in prison, where they make up an astonishing 24 percent of the state's prisoners.

Mayor Rudolph Giuliani even made defiance of the country's immigration rules a rallying cry of his administration. A 1996 federal welfare law declared that no local government could prohibit its employees from cooperating with the INS. Mayor Giuliani spent city tax dollars to challenge the law in court. When he lost the case, he vowed to preserve the spirit of the sanctuary policy by notifying city workers that they weren't obligated to cooperate.

We have now learned that indifference to the laws of this country has a cost. September 11 ringleader Mohamed Atta got back into the country after overstaying his previous visa, which he shouldn't have been granted in the first place, since he had previously met with Iraqi intelligence officials. Previous terrorists have found safe harbor in New York despite being in the country illegally: Mahmud Abouhalima, one of the masterminds of the 1993 World Trade Center attack, got a hack license from the Taxi and Limousine Commission in 1986, even though his visa had expired. By the time he fraudulently got a green card in 1999, under an amnesty program for farmworkers, he had already begun collaborating with El Sayed Al Nosair, the assassin of Rabbi Meir Kahane and collaborator in the 1993 Trade Center attack.

Albany legislators should quickly pass a spate of long-ignored bills, many sponsored by State Senator Frank Padavan, cracking down on immigration fraud. A top priority should be to forbid undocumented aliens from attending state universities and to require those schools to verify the legal status of all students. Also essential are proposed laws requiring police agencies to cooperate with the INS and forbidding the issuance of driver's licenses to illegal aliens. Nationally the country needs to implement an electronic identification card, encoding biometric information like fingerprints to prevent immigration and identity fraud.

Though intelligence is the best weapon against terrorism,

physical security in buildings and public spaces needs strengthening as well. Manhattan needs far better screening at its bridges and tunnels to prevent truck bombs from entering the city; that means finally requiring all truck deliveries to be made at night, over dedicated bridges with far tighter security checks than currently exist. The city's traffic congestion would be immeasurably improved, and the extra cost in services and goods would be easily recovered in greater citizen confidence and improved mobility.

Given the ready availability of bomb ingredients, some truck bombs may be manufactured within Manhattan to avoid detection. Landmark buildings should be protected by concrete bollards or planters at the perimeter to fend off vehicle access; trucks making deliveries should be thoroughly inspected outside the building and their delivery status verified before they enter any loading docks.

Increased patrol presence in Manhattan should be maintained indefinitely, both to deter crime and to boost public confidence. Any uniformed officers still holding desk jobs that could be handled by civilians should be on the streets; the city should revise any union rules to the contrary. Patrols with bomb-sniffing dogs should become routine in crowded areas and in subway stations.

The price tag for protecting the city against future attacks will be high. New York will have to revamp its traditional priorities; it can no longer afford to maintain a cradle-to-grave welfare state that rewards dysfunction and penalizes productivity. Private business will face higher security costs to maintain a Manhattan location; couple that additional spending with the city's sky-high taxes, and many businesses will decide to decamp (or never come in the first place). To prevent that exodus, the city must avoid any tax increases—or, better yet, lower taxes. It can only do so, given the expense of heightened security, by cutting spending in other areas.

Eight years ago no one would have believed that the NYPD could possibly cut crime by 60 percent—but it did. There is no reason to fear that it cannot rise to this challenge as well.

How the Racial Profiling Myth Helps Terrorists

I'VE BEEN AMUSING MYSELF recently with the following experiment: I call up the most strident anti-police activists of recent years—including Washington's local police scourge, Georgetown law professor David Cole, who argues that every aspect of the criminal justice system is racist. I ask these police critics the following question: Suppose that in the wake of September 11, the FBI decides to check out recent graduates of American flight schools to see who else may be plotting to use airplanes as weapons. Which students, I ask, should the FBI investigate: all of the would-be pilots, or a subset of them?

Without exception, I get the following answer: "The FBI should investigate everyone."

"Everyone?" I respond. "That's a big number. You'd be stretching the resources of the FBI dangerously thin. Wouldn't you look," I ask, "at a student from Saudi Arabia more closely than at someone from Kentucky?"

Nope, comes the reply. The FBI has to investigate everyone equally to avoid racism. A civil liberties law professor from St. Louis University even insisted, "I'm sure the FBI has the resources to investigate everybody."

From my experiment I have concluded, first, that these self-described policing experts know absolutely nothing about police work. Any police investigation has to use known facts to narrow the scope of the inquiry, since manpower is finite. In this case the FBI would be irresponsible not to use the nationalities and religious identities of the nineteen hijackers to search for their co-conspirators among flight-school alumni: the hijackers themselves, after all, defined their mission in religious terms. Yet despite their obvious ignorance, the police critics in my survey, and others like them, have controlled the public discourse about law enforcement for the last half-decade, creating a policy and public relations nightmare for cops.

I also conclude from my experiment that if these professional police-bashers exert the same influence over counterterrorism as they have over domestic policing, we're all in trouble. Indeed, we probably already missed an opportunity to avoid the terror of 9/11 because of their baneful effects. In 1996 Vice President Al Gore chaired a commission on aviation security to strengthen airline defenses against terrorism. When word leaked out that the commission was considering a profiling system that would take into account a passenger's national origin and ethnicity, among other factors, in assessing the security risk he posed, anti-law-enforcement advocates, along with the Arab lobby, went ballistic. The counsel for the ACLU fired off an op-ed to the *Washington Post* complaining that "profiles select people who fit the stereotype of a terrorist. They frequently discriminate on the basis of race, religion or national origin."

At the terms "stereotype" and "discriminate," the reader was supposed to shriek in revulsion and march on the FAA in protest. But can we turn off our exquisitely sensitive racism radar for a moment and consider the question of terrorist profiles with cold reason? The ACLU's counsel complains that "profiles select people who fit the stereotype of a terrorist." But a stereotype in this case is nothing more than a compilation of facts about who has attacked American interests in the past and who, given what we know about the networks that promote anti-American terrorism, is most likely to do so in the future. It is al-Qaida and its brethren that have defined themselves by religion and regional interest, not American law enforcement.

In fact, racial profiling, as the cop-bashers define it—and they are the only ones to define it, since the police have never endorsed the term—is irrelevant to the hunt for terrorists. As the cop-bashers imagine it, racial profiling is simply about playing the odds. If the police, based on crime statistics, believe that blacks are more likely to commit armed robbery than whites, they will pat down a black person, according to the ACLU, merely on the chance that he is carrying a gun. But beyond mere numerical odds, there is no inherent connection between race and robbery. Whites may commit proportionally less robbery than blacks, but commit it they do.

Islamic anti-American terrorism, by contrast, is by its very definition perpetrated by radical Muslims to avenge American imperialism in the Middle East. If we concentrate our investigation on Middle Eastern Muslims, we are not playing the odds: we are following the terrorists' own self-definition. We run virtually no risk of overlooking terrorists if our investigation ignores Unitarians from Minnesota; whereas police will certainly overlook robbers if they never consider whites as suspects.

Such hard truths about the terrorist threat, however, violate the central precept of our modern discourse about crime and law enforcement: that all groups commit crime or terrorism at equal rates. So the Gore Commission dutifully abjured the inclusion of national origin, religion, ethnicity, and even gender in its recommended passenger profiling system. The result—the Computer-Assisted Passenger Profiling System (CAPPS)—omits precisely those criteria that are the major predictors of anti-American terrorism. Instead, CAPPS looks only at such circumstances as paying cash for tickets and buying one-way routes—behavior that terrorists can easily change.

The anti-law-enforcement ethos of the time hampered the

terrorist-fighting potential of CAPPS even further. Because questioning or searching someone was now seen as akin to brutality—even, apparently, when performed by private security guards—the CAPPS system would be used only to screen checked luggage; the owner of that luggage would not himself be searched, for that would be discriminatory. Sadly, Energy Secretary Spencer Abraham has encouraged this absurd notion that searching someone's luggage at an airport is a frightening exercise of police power. Abraham, who is of Lebanese descent, told the *Wall Street Journal* that after the 1996 and 1998 terrorist attacks against U.S. interests in Saudi Arabia and Africa, his carry-on luggage was searched a "disproportionate" number of times. It would have been "scary," he said, had he not had a Senate ID card, and he complained twice to Attorney General Janet Reno.

Now, maybe I'm just an extremely courageous person, but my luggage has been searched at airports without filling me with fear. I wish Secretary Abraham would try balancing the trauma of being asked to open his briefcase against the potential annihilation of American cities.

Had a fully rational profiling system that takes advantage of everything we know about anti-American terrorism been put into place instead of CAPPS, the September 11 plot might have been foiled. As it happened, CAPPS flagged two of the September 11 terrorists that day, presumably because of their travel itineraries and method of payment; but, consistent with the rules of the system, only their checked luggage was scrutinized. Had they themselves been searched, security officials may have wondered why two Arab men already under suspicion were carrying box-cutters, and looked further.

After CAPPS was up and running, as the hijackers were learning to fly and casing their targets, the promoters of the fiction that all groups commit crime and terrorism equally kept up the pressure. Hussein Ibish of the Arab-American Anti-Discrimination

Committee fumed in early 2000 that Americans were really hung up on this silly notion of Islamic terrorism. "Shadowy Arabs and Middle East terrorism fit into the mind of the media," he sneered. Of course, an Algerian had just been caught with explosives to blow up the Los Angeles International Airport to mark the new millennium, and Jordan had foiled other millennial plots against American interests in the Middle East. But we can't notice those facts, since doing so would contribute to stereotypes.

Islamic advocacy groups also incessantly complained about airport searches. The Department of Transportation penitentially ordered an audit of airline security checks, even though in all of 2000 only fifteen Arab-Americans actually filed discrimination complaints. The results of that audit, performed in June 2001 at the Detroit airport, remain a secret. It's not hard to guess why.

Let's assume that the audit shows that CAPPS still disproportionately selects people of Arab ancestry, since it does flag passengers who have traveled frequently to terrorist-sponsoring states. Under the logic of the equal crime and terrorism fiction, the FAA would have to discard that travel criterion, since it is unacceptable that any group be shown to have a greater likelihood of terrorist associations than any other group. Before September 11 it is quite conceivable that the FAA would indeed have monkeyed with its passenger screening system until it created something that flags all groups equally.

Doing so, of course, would mean purging CAPPS of any remaining factors that actually do predict terrorism. No big deal— police and fire departments have long been forced by the federal government to discard any job requirements that conflict with the goal of proportional racial representation. But after September 11 the FAA may be a little less willing to sacrifice safety for political correctness, so it is simply keeping the audit under wraps.

If the FAA is having second thoughts about the imperatives of the anti-law-enforcement agenda, the primary keepers of that agenda have been totally unfazed by September 11. No sooner did the FBI begin investigating the attacks than cries over racial profiling swelled, enthusiastically amplified by the mainstream media.

On September 21, 2001, the *New York Times* quoted unnamed civil liberties lawyers who complained that "there are signs of profiling in the pattern of arrests so far." In other words, only racism could explain those arrests. Absent FBI bias, the *Times's* sources imply, terrorist suspects would come in a rainbow of religions, nationalities, and ethnicities—because, as we all know, all groups are equally likely to commit crime or terrorism.

I asked University of Toledo law professor David Harris, the most strident of the anti–racial profiling crusaders, whether the New York police could rationally choose whether to focus their terrorism intelligence gathering on mosques in Brooklyn or Catholic churches in Queens. He ducked the question. "Why would I want to speculate on that?" he answered.

I asked discrimination law professor Melissa Cole if there's an equal chance of a Scandinavian and Arab Islamic cell member committing terrorism. "I don't see why not," she said brightly. "Just because it's never happened before, doesn't mean [the Scandinavians] are not the next ones to commit a terrorist act." This kind of radical skepticism may be fine for a freshman philosophy paper, but law professors should know better. It is irresponsible to argue that our severely limited resources for tracking down terrorists should be spread evenly across society.

The hyperbole of contemporary police-bashing also survived the terrorist destruction intact. Within twenty-four hours of the World Trade Center's collapse, newspapers and TV stations across the country started comparing America's likely response to the attack to the mass internment of Japanese Americans in World War II. One of my favorite headlines came from the September 24 *New York Times*: "War on Terrorism Stirs Memories of Internment"— this at a time when the government had detained seventy-five immigrants, or 0.002 percent of the country's Arab population. At the close of 2001 the cumulative total of detainees was a little over one thousand, or 0.025 percent of the Arab-American population. A "vast dragnet," screamed the *New York Times*. I think it unlikely that we will be reading about mass deportations any time soon.

Eclipsing the fury over the detention of suspects, however, was the uproar over Attorney General John Ashcroft's plan to interview five thousand young males who had arrived from terror-sponsoring states over the last two years—some 0.1 percent of the Arab-American population. A "dragnet approach that is likely to magnify concerns of racial and ethnic profiling," brayed the ACLU. Not a day passed when the media did not righteously report the indignation and supposed panic that this plan stirred in the Muslim community. The chair of the Islamic Mission of America denounced it as "encroaching on my civil liberties." Hussein Ibish of the Arab-American Anti-Discrimination Committee compared it to McCarthyism—always a crowd-pleasing analogy with the left.

Time for a reality check. Being interviewed in a noncustodial setting by the police, with the option to cut off the interview at any time, is very far from constituting a violation of civil liberties. No one has a right not ever to be asked a question by the police. (Of course, the immigrants whom Ashcroft wants to talk to are not even American citizens, but we'll leave that objection aside.) If such voluntary interviews were the constitutional enormity that the press implies, no crime could ever be solved; the police have always canvassed local communities for leads in serious felonies. Now, however, the anti-law-enforcement lobby and Muslim advocates want to deny the FBI that basic law-enforcement tool after the bloodiest crime ever committed on American soil. What would the ACLU and the Arab lobby have the government do—sit back and just hope that no one is planning another catastrophic attack?

Perhaps if the spokesmen for the Muslim and Arab communities had exhorted their people to come forward and help the government early on, the FBI would not need its canvas. But from 9/11 forward, the most vocal Arab-American and Muslim leaders have played victim politics, portraying the Arab-American community as the object of American bigotry rather than as a willing and essential ally in the war on terror. They have done so by exploiting the twin pillars of contemporary anti-police rhetoric—the fiction that all groups commit crime at equal rates and the hyperbole that casts any action by the police—any questioning or investigation whatsoever—as hostile and lawless. It is high time for Arab-American leaders to change their tune, calling for maximum cooperation with the terrorist investigation as the patriotic duty of every Muslim and Arab-American. Don't count on it, though.

There is a lesson to be drawn from our current predicament: bad ideas have consequences. We let them fester at our own risk.

As the campaign against the police gathered steam in the 1990s, few people spoke up against it or tried to understand the complexities of policing that the anti-profiling crusade ignores. Swearing opposition to racial profiling—and thereby implying its existence—became an easy way to show one's racial good faith, even if the swearer had not the slightest idea whether cops really practiced it. And now a construct that was bogus from the start is intruding itself into a battle even more serious than the war on crime.

Before September 11 certain culture-war disputes were beginning to seem routine and futile in their ritualistic repetition: the battles over the multicultural curriculum, for instance, or victim politics. Now we see that such disputes are matters of life and death.

2002

Index

A NOTE ON THE AUTHOR

Heather Mac Donald received her B.A. in English from Yale University, graduating summa cum laude with a Mellon Fellowship to Cambridge University, where she earned her M.A. in English. Later she received a J.D. from the Stanford University Law School. A nonpracticing lawyer, Ms. Mac Donald has clerked for the Honorable Stephen Reinhardt in the United States Court of Appeals for the Ninth Circuit; has been an attorney-adviser in the office of the general counsel for the United States Environmental Protection Agency; and has volunteered with the National Resource Defense Counsel in New York City. She is the author of *The Burden of Bad Ideas*, and her writings have appeared in *City Journal*, the *Wall Street Journal*, the *Washington Post*, the *New York Times*, the *New York Post*, *The New Republic*, *Partisan Review*, *The New Criterion*, *The Public Interest*, and *Academic Questions*. She is currently a John M. Olin Fellow at The Manhattan Institute and a contributing editor to *City Journal*. She lives and works in New York City.